MALVINA PRUDENCE TCHAPDA

My brain attack

MALVINA PRUDENCE TCHAPDA

My brain attack

JustFiction Edition

Imprint
Any brand names and product names mentioned in this book are subject to trademark, brand or patent protection and are trademarks or registered trademarks of their respective holders. The use of brand names, product names, common names, trade names, product descriptions etc. even without a particular marking in this work is in no way to be construed to mean that such names may be regarded as unrestricted in respect of trademark and brand protection legislation and could thus be used by anyone.

Cover image: Provided by the author

Publisher:
JustFiction! Edition
is a trademark of
Dodo Books Indian Ocean Ltd., member of the OmniScriptum S.R.L Publishing group
str. A.Russo 15, of. 61, Chisinau-2068, Republic of Moldova Europe
Printed at: see last page
ISBN: 978-620-3-57750-1

Copyright © MALVINA PRUDENCE TCHAPDA
Copyright © 2021 Dodo Books Indian Ocean Ltd., member of the OmniScriptum S.R.L Publishing group

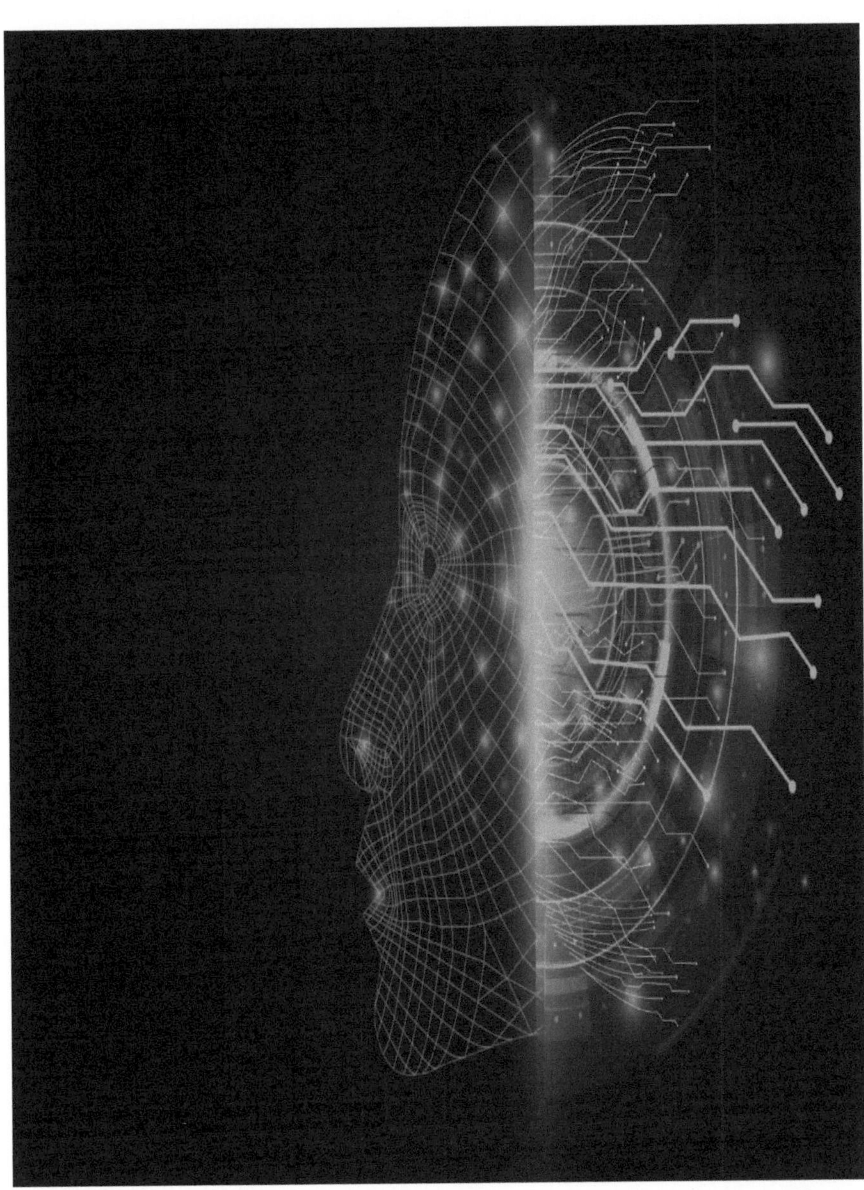

My Brain Attack.

How to Contact:

+237 699 176 907;
Tcheuko.26@gmail.com
Facebook: Malvina Tchapda

Contents

<u>My brain attack by Miss TCHEUKO TCHAPDA MALVINA PRUDENCE.</u>

It is 9:09 am on 08/20/2021 when I pick up my pen to start writing my story:

This is the life of a young woman with a bright future, a future turned upside down by human oppression. She lives with an open brain inclined to electronic manipulations; trying to go up the slope, it is with divine help that she will get her head out of the water.

We come with a story never seen or experienced on planet Earth.

A story known by everyone around the world.

It's the history of a young woman with a promising future who was victim and who lives with her brain (open) within everyone's reach.

By electronic machinery, criminals have access to the data of her head, her brain. I talk about her thoughts, her dreams, her past life, her future life by the minute and by the week, her daily life, her body and even heart rate, her organs and intestines...

They also have access to her whole body, they have this opportunity to bring in and out informations or datas and abuse her. Those informations or datas take the form of videos, voices or audio or sounds, smells, bad or good air, injections, bites, attacks, insults, stretching of nerves and organs, the worst visual monstrosities that can exist.

Having heard of this, the return from her family and entourage were silent, encouraging and violent reactions.

Knowing that what she was experiencing crossed borders, the sounds and calls came from everywhere and the interventions were of several types and nature
. What is mind boggling is the way they intervene, through shadows passing in front of you and around you. Some of them speaking on television without any normal contact.
Driven by the desire to make her dreams come true, to regain a healthy life, to free herself from her

oppressors, she wishes to share her story and therefore denounce this criminal act which, moreover, would have been punished. The latter made her the victim of harassment, invasion of her privacy, violation of her right to sleep, theft of his intellectual property, bodily harm, invasion of home privacy; moreover, her privacy, her tranquility, her human rights are being violated. Finally, it even generated a shortfall over the course of my life.

Such an act that violates human rights and intellectual property rights deserves to be denounced and punished. This young woman is me, what if it was you?

We therefore want to highlight:

- The inhuman nature of cervical piracy.

- The fact knowned internationally.

- Description and understanding of this instrument.

- Daily manifestations: physical abuse, around me, images of days and nights.

- The continuity of the most recent images.

- The difficulties she had to face.

- The efforts deployed and put in place against this scourge.

- The attempts, The cooperation, the understanding and kindness of the men of the shadows.

- Denounce these criminal acts.

- The consequences of such a practice on everyday life and on the future.

- The attitudes to have when faced with this kind of act.

THE INHUMAN NATURE OF CERVICAL PIRACY.

The parts that make up the head of a human being are very important for the entire human body. The head is one of the basic organs. She is the one who makes the discussion via a simple path: reception of the message - analysis or reflection - constitution of a final idea - return of the message through words or gestures. So you can't touch it any way, nor cross it electronically. It is a notorious and indisputable inhumanity.

The head and the ideas it carries boost morale. This morale added to the breath of life generates the smile or the tears. And therefore human beings need a solid morale to move forward in their life and in their daily life.

Also, it is this head that produces the works of the spirit. Intellectual property only has meaning when the work of ideas has a design-build approach. It is the head that creates and shapes the concepts. The world and systems have been built by the intellect of famous men and women, by visionaries. They gave their heads, put their brains to work, developed concepts. So we see the inhumanly criminal side of whoever touches or enters it electronically. This is an absolute criminality.

You will agree that the greatest literary feats, the constructions of great buildings, of great empires, the great vehicles brands, the greatest managerial tools in the world, the great models of medicine, the means to soften manners, the greatest systems ever designed are the works of the mind and the results of the head.

Thinking equal innovating, in all aspects of life. Everything we do comes from thought, from human thought.

Thoughts, ideas, the head appear to be a source of income. We know that the performance of any function is based on the fruit of the imagination or the ability to analyze and understand.

And therefore, bandits and criminals should not have access to it arbitrarily at the risk of being accused of undermining the construction of intellectual achievement.

My brain attack by Miss TCHEUKO TCHAPDA MALVINA PRUDENCE.

Just because we recognize heads that are the source of
unproductivity, we should not touch or overwhelm heads
and brains that generate beautiful things, things that
can be exploited.

As for the body which preserves our physical strength,
that strength is necessary to live and without which no
one can have peace of mind on a daily basis. Therefore
bodily disturbance should in no case be suffered by a
human being; moreover without being declared ill.
Everyone loves to have good health
. Everyone likes to say "I am in good shape." And
therefore to be abused electronically is a human rights
violation. It is dehumanizing the body and its system so
much that it is not an object or an animal or a connected
toy. Warming up the body with a bad idea should be
condemned because it is bad. Torturing a human being
electronically is never allowed, especially when the
human being has done nothing wrong.

Being in good shape is very necessary for a human being.
Having that intention to take it away is to take away the
smile, the joy of life, and it is to penalize the others
who need him, who care about him. The Sacramento of the
human body does not allow this. It is often said that the
body is the temple of the Lord and no one should use it
for the wrong reasons. He is the divine representation
therefore he should be kept according to the divine
precepts.

The scarcity of health makes it impossible to grant the
slightest indulgence to these hacking practices. The
divine privilege of health and fitness does not allow one
to be flexible in the face of head or body hacking. The
race for health, the fragility of the body's organs and
the perpetual quest for physical form require such great
effort that it is unacceptable that an individual can
satisfy the desire to harm a body. Health therefore has a
sacred character. Many of them are in hospitals hoping to
get out; a thief cannot take the initiative to fill
hospital rooms and clinics because of inhumane
intentions.
The body is a divine property. It's no coincidence that
there is a limit. It is not insignificant that the Lord

has covered it like the blood and the sex which is extracted only with consent. Without undressing people walk naked? No it's not tolerable.

In addition, there are people who live from their physical form. There are some who sell it, who market it. Like my ideas, their physical form is their breadwinner. Industries turn because of the productivity that comes with it. So no one can prevent others from making money and in turn participating in the developments of the sectors.
So to attain the mental and physical forms of a human being is depravity. To go so far as to overwhelm her, to torture her is dehumanization, intolerable though it is.

THE FACT KNOWNED INTERNATIONALLY.

When I saw the facts and confirmed my suspicions, which facts and suspicions revolve around the hacked nature of my brain, the fact of being connected to an electronic device, that my life was the subject of comments and appreciations by more than one. Others who spoke at the same time as me, others who repeated what i was saying. Hearing the names of my friends, relatives and acquaintances come out of the mouths of passers-by and those who did not know; that already testified to me being famous. I like to point out: known despite myself. A bizarre remark was to realize that as much as my life, my daily life was also subject to comment. My alarm clock, my breakfast, my market, my cooking, my lunch and supper; my exchanges and discussion too. The reality is that no one has ever experienced this. I have not yet hear that you enter a person's life so deeply; internationally recognized. Most of the time this one or that one is seen outside his house or has chosen to sign a contract for a reality TV show. Otherwise, apart from me, we have never heard that everyday life, breathing, thoughts, actions and even toilet visits specific to a person are so watched and moreover subject to comments.

I noticed the evolving aspect of hostilities as I heard our names in songs. Our names sung and infiltrated by internationally renowned singers. My name and those of the other friends were sung. Oohhh la la! Some were rather distinguished for the kind messages they reached us. After reflection, these were the singers that I liked or that I had to appreciate in my book of life. In other words, it was about singers we use to see, like and appreciate on the reading my hacked brain was offering.

As soon as I saw my dress on television, more precisely the patterns of my floral dress in white and pink colors. These same patterns of dress were worn by a TV star, a world famous star, very famous and talented. Sometimes I would find some of my words on shows of several genres. Repeating exactly what I said to people or what I wrote.

Some of them gave me the name Malvinajeep.

We were in the middle of Corona Virus pandemic, like vaccinations and protection, things were going just as quickly.

Seeing this, Malvinajeep wondered why nothing was done. Why will I remain in this situation, deplorable it may be? A very surprising and unique case, a salutary cause.

I got little lucky when I felt desired and wanted interventions from certain people. These speakers were foreigners. I will call them The Henchmen. They called me Malvinajeep. They mobilized for my cause, my situation, my hacked head and my connected body. Demonstrating the desire to take me by plane, they wanted to multiply other actions: throwing a suitcase, reaching me in hotels or even passing me an envelope under a hotel room door, reaching me by mail or account banking….

There were these men who were trying to manifest their presence by sending their shadows. That's why I'll call them The Shadow Men. Through their shadows, I could perceive their gestures when they wanted it of course. They wanted to send me messages and instructions on when and how they would come and take me by plane. I have this vague feeling that they really wanted to achieve this goal but didn't get it.

The messages continued on television. Through a series, a show, a football game, I had at least one person who wanted to let me know something. Whether it is on the situation in general, on my clothing, on the question of whether I knew them, or even on my difficulty. There was like a bizarrely described interplay between my thoughts, my smile, my gestures, the applause, my jubilee and these international guests. It's clear they wanted to be there; it was enough to find a way. Also, they wanted this situation solved and completed.

Most disturbing of all were the sounds and voices all around my household. These noises and ways had multiple authors. I have toured three houses in two years that I endured them each time. Here, I heard that the mobilizations were from several sources and orders. Bringing together actors, singers, foreign representatives, human rights defenders and many others. In addition to commenting on my daily life, my thoughts, my actions, noises and voices helped me the actions of others, these international stakeholders. These noises and voices went so far as to tell me what would happen tomorrow, in the near and far future. How did they know that? It's about the mids weren't there, no, they weren't involved. How did they know that? There is a device, an instrument which simply makes it possible to know what will happen tomorrow.

As I write noises are erupting from all around me asking for a tale of how I experienced things and to know what they didn't know about me or this sadly lived story. And it is with pleasure that I give them satisfaction.

<u>**My brain attack by Miss TCHEUKO TCHAPDA MALVINA PRUDENCE.**</u>

DESCRIPTION AND UNDERSTANDING OF THIS INSTRUMENT.

I was subject to manipulation by a device or instrument. To have undergone and function of the explanations which reached me, I will recognize its functionalities. You could see the past, present and tomorrow. Also, it was possible to feel the effects of touch. A third is this potentiality to emit noises and sounds all around due to the connection of your physic. A fourth is the question-answer sequence on a machine.

Without having the precision on everything to hold in hand. I bring you the descriptive contingencies of the results of these machines.

First of all to this device which reads everything, in particular the past, the present and the tomorrow, of which three are known or existing. The past that I call **P**, the present **a** and the following days **B**. Because we saw a tomorrow, a **B**, personally I thought of a link, a kind of unknown, another experience that would allow the realization of **B**. I associated an unknown (**x**) with the possibility of modeling / malleable. The set therefore involves recognizing a process which looks like an equational formula **a + x = B**.

P is the past. This instrument can appear as a kind of time travel, being able to retrace your past and lived deeds and gestures, this in the most unimaginable details. The **P** was made up of your previous life, the life before the **a** regardless of the years, months, weeks, hours, or seconds before. Everything you know you have experienced in the past is there. I'm talking about your good and bad times, your beautiful and mistakes in dating, friendship, your kind and awkward habits including all the places you have been around ... This **P** also contains and very oddly your ideas and thoughts regardless of the distance temporal spacio. I'm talking about all the ideas that have crossed your mind, inherent in your brain or not.

a is the existing, the daily in the present moment, the current daily life, the air breathed, the lived second, the palpable minute, the concrete hour. This device made it possible to see all that. This is how you could see everything I was doing down to the minute. Instantly, you read my thoughts, my words, my exchanges with the entourage I was seeing at the time. Whatever path I took, wherever I was, it was accessible. I'm talking about the house, kitchen, bedroom, toilet, office, church, all the routes taken, even the road, hairdresser, weddings, restaurants… Everything I did and thought about was watched.

B is the next day, the next moment in seconds, in minutes, in hours and days, in months and years. Everything I will do tomorrow, and what I could potentially do. I speak of potentiality because there were multiple paths to take depending on the opportunities that presented themselves. This is how my next minute was read. My coming hour was known. My days and months that followed could be seen and known. So you could see who would date me, who I would work with, who I would meet and what I would do as a result. Depending on the path taken, we had a lineage and a visible continuation, it was enough that he had acceptance between me and the other element of the path. About me, my professional life, my future dating, my realizations, my anger and even weeding where I was invited. These appear in the plural for the simple reason that the possibilities presented themselves depending on who approached me.

All these results to whom I will assign title to the property. Yes, we could recognize them a title of owner to those who were there because there are some that do not appear there and there are lines that did not cross or I would say paths that did not break through.

x it is missing and not yet produced which gave birth to the **B**. It appears very donefull since the **B** has taken place. Because between this **a** and **B** I recognized a link. Logically, if there was a result in the curve the next day, something had to spark it. Beside the element of will or mutual acceptance, this **x** was an initiative coming from you or from a third person in connection or not with what was being seen. It can be the sending of a

<u>My brain attack by Miss TCHEUKO TCHAPDA MALVINA PRUDENCE.</u>

letter or mail, instructions and actions, the provision
of a car, a plane or a vehicle for transport, a seat or
meeting, a phone call or a message, a marriage proposal…
This **x** is a set of initiatives and possible and
authorized facts which led to these known and known
tomorrows.

This same **x** takes a capital place when the **B** appears less
favorable. It would suffice to learn a little about the
daily, about the **a**, or to refrain from doing what would
be harmful. What **x** that made so much noise and shook more
than one, difficult for some to apprehend; forcing others
to calm for who saw the negative results, inglorious, not
happy.

I say results because it was about a well-defined and
almost certain causal link, we know all being causality
around us. It is indeed this missing element necessary to
reach or achieve this **B** which was already known or read.
Among these x's, there are some that may be near, others
far. There are some that depend on you, on me and others
not. And of course when he depends on another person, he
sees himself the risk of being slowed down or even
blocked by factors such as deterrence, resentment,
jealousy, distraction of intention….

Where appropriate, I nourish this idea that my **x** is to
speak to you, to speak in these very selected, sincere,
intended to be instructive and constructive and anxious
terms.

Those with the **P, a,** Q&A thought that discussion or
physical presence could be done without or bypassed. But
no. It remained essential and unavoidable. The normal
course of events had to continue to be respected. The
order of life should never cease to be the basis.

There was even a pushy, cartoonish version that stood out
...

I will recognize a significant link between the **P** and the
a. The daily life which is furnished by the part of
dating, relationships with others is likely to take a
hit. Thus, after having delved into this part of the
other's life, judgments and looks can change (wrongly or

if acceptable depending on the degrees of nervousness felt), so also attitudes. It was this consequence that gave rise to the unauthorized nature of the use of this instrument. The risk of damage is great and sometimes disproportionate. This influence of P giving rise to a happier **a** or not, everything depends on the degree of neutrality or consideration experienced. Without recounting your past life, we had access to it. Even if it is recognized the need to explain the contents of this **P;** explanation that only the owner of the deeds could give.

Likewise, by extension there was a connection between the **P** and the **B.** To the extent that everyday life might change because of what had been seen in the **P,** the future is likely to take a hit. This is how there are those who no longer speak to each other, who are no longer in contact in the next day's book, in the **B** because of what happened in the watched **P.**
Another feature allowed them to connect and touch my organs. From head to toe I felt the effects of the beatings, stings, injections and abuse that I was subjected to electronically. I don't know how it was possible to do this but I was sure of the sensory effects as they were very painful. Likewise, the unwanted effects of a foreign substance introduced electronically came to me physically. Sometimes these sensations stopped and I deduce from the disconnection of my electronicized self. Distinct from sensations from blows or the like, there were some that were prolonged, sensations after stings or injections. These came to life in every part of my body without exception. And that's how I smelled odors they sent me. The most curious was when I sniffed the scents of another person. So there was this possibility of connecting other people and smelling each other's scents. The weirdest thing is the possibility of closing your eyes and transcribing images and voices into another person's head at will. So a person is calmly at home and sees images appearing in his head from the head or at the initiative of another person. Likewise with voices, in the throat there comes in a concealed way what another person has introduced. This device is not very clean, its usefulness does not bode very well I find.

My brain attack by Miss TCHEUKO TCHAPDA MALVINA PRUDENCE.

Thirdly, from this device emerged the potential to emit
noises and sounds all around for the simple connection.
By what machinery I do not know, around, I heard
pronunciations and words of the people who had connected
me to their machine. It could have been a tablet or a
phone, I have no idea. This is how all parts of the
house, wherever I went that had a roof, were crossed by
high or low pitched voices depending on how loud it was.
What surprised me the most was when I was in places
without roofs. Similar voices were possible; I concluded
that just connecting me was causing all of this.

The fourth observation was the question-answer sequence
on a machine. It appears from users' accounts that I was
asked questions and the answers followed. There was a
possibility of verbal exchange without human initiative,
without making contact, without seeing each other. As
surprising as it is, people asked me questions without
calling me, or seeing me, or without me speaking
humanely; and they were getting responses almost similar
to what I would get if I was in-person. As proof, the
answers reached me around my house and I recognized my
outbursts of thoughts and arguments among. Clearly, a
device that traces my naturalness and impulses of ideas.
And so we could see there the naturalness of people was
it virtuous, gentle, lenient, angry, machiavellian too.
Any kind of answers could come from it, whether they
related to your personal life, your past, your opinion of
a person or something, your wish and desire.

<u>My brain attack by Miss TCHEUKO TCHAPDA MALVINA PRUDENCE.</u>

DAILY MANIFESTATIONS: PHYSICAL ABUSE, AROUND ME, IMAGES OF DAYS AND NIGHTS.

These demonstrations are presented and revolve around three salient facts: physical abuse, the reactions of people around me and the images that I constantly saw.

It all started when I finally went home, left the family home to gain autonomy and experience its joys. I lived in a dorm room and went about my daily routine. Metro - work - sleep as one would say. By this time I had gotten used to the pace since I didn't report any major concerns. It's true I was single, I didn't have a boyfriend. My darling at that time was my job. Work that I tried to do brilliantly, with passion, dedication and professionalism. I had signed a temporary contract in a local company where I held the position of "Customer care". I wasn't complaining. I loved work very much. A very professional and pleasant work environment. I was hooked and dedicated to it yet it would allow me to build a career. I devoted myself to it very early in the morning and finished in the evening. The working hours gave us an hour of break during which I savored my small dishes. I used to go out and sit on a bench outside the building.

As soon as I finished the evening shift, I headed home, had dinner and fell asleep. After my prayer, I fell asleep peacefully, I remember it very well. In the morning I would put my breakfast in a bowl, then my lunch in another and I went to my work. Such was the outline of my days, of my daily life. I was quite satisfied and happy with it.

Everything was going relatively well when suddenly during a night's sleep I had a nightmare. At that time, I was talking about a nightmare. It was by dint of having them over and over that I concluded the idea of inserting images into my head when I slept. That night I saw a man stomping his foot hard in the sand, raising the dust. From that night on, it was a succession of images and scenes that were not clean. These were unusual and new. They looked with confirmation like montages or pre-recorded. I saw roosters, hens running. Evildoers were sending me disguised monsters in my head repelling and frightening those who wanted to help me.

They were not welcome because they did not emanate from me, nor from my sleep. Through reflection, I came to the conclusion that someone was inserting obscenities in my brain while sleeping. I saw ugly scenes from people I knew; in this case colleagues and friends. One of the things that struck me as weird was that I was seeing professional acquaintances from five years ago. Over several nights I had very obscene images of them in un-Catholic contexts which I don't think looked like them at all. Imagine, you had to go back and work with them each time. You see the daily life, saying Hello, handing over such a document, smiling ... It was very difficult.

These images were associated with odors. Once I needed to rest; so I took advantage of the break granted and I bent down on my worktable. Suddenly a strong odor came out, a smell similar to urine. Here begins Another highlight of this disaster. These were the smells sent to me. The smells reached me at the edge of the pool. I felt these smells in front and behind. I was very scared of it. As a woman it was not normal. I rushed to the bathroom to undress and do an inspection of the genital walls, but I didn't inhale the same scents. Everything here was neutral. I repeated the same checking process at home but nothing continued in terms of foul odors.

Without waiting, I called the family doctor: Dr Sam. The goal was to get diagnosed because I couldn't stay with these smells anymore. I wanted to clear up the ambiguity. My health is a priority with me, we know it as the first asset of a human being. And so the doctor came to my house to take samples from me. A few days after his results showed typhoid. To my surprise I looked for the link with these smells without finding. My treatment was combined with antibiotics and vaginal eggs. It was with a big pleasure that I consumed them because it is one of my privileged moments: to heal oneself and to pursue the quest for health and well-being. And while I was on my treatment, I still sniffed the scents and was almost desperate even though I had nothing to do with it. These smells were present at work and at home. I remember I was afraid to walk around people at my place of duty for fear of being inhaled. But hey, it was about moving forward with the conviction that a human body was far from producing so much catastrophe in the air.

Comes the end of my treatment and still suffered from the same attacks. Whose initiative was it? Until today I never knew.

After that I had a boyfriend, with whom we decided to marry for life, a proper marriage in fact. Everywhere we went I received the scents: in the car, at the restaurant, to my family in-laws, at my parents it was the same. I didn't understand anything at all. Then from mu analysis, I came to the conclusion that this was some kind of attack. The goal was to discredit me with my people and make me uncomfortable wherever I went. Fortunately the scents were centered only on me and around me. But it wasn't always a person's business when I was in an air-conditioned room with people around. The smell spread and I noticed the behaviors of people around me or who had been sitting for almost months. So my reaction was to get up immediately and go to the bathroom or walk away. And as soon as I took that attitude, those smells would go away. It was this in and out that made me calm down and not question my feminine hygiene. I continued to trust myself and my privacy. We all know how important our private parts are to us women.

The worst thing was to be subjected to these scent jets at work and in the middle of people. The odors varied ,in front of it was urine and behind it was toilets, salts. But who was so angry with me? Everything suggests that criminals did not want me to work or get married. But I did not let myself be overwhelmed by this, although it was very serious and picturesque. I was continuing my life line, remember I continued to trust me.

Now is the time to have a baby, since the future husband was going to travel to the Europe. At my suggestion, we planned to do pre-marital exams. As is always the case and highly recommended before marriage or sex. In any case, this is a crucial and essential step when dating a man. No sooner said than done. We went to one of the famous laboratory in the city, rather sophisticated and very recommendable. I was excited about it because I love this part of the relationship. I like to feel healthy and mobilize what it takes to. And I will add that this was a renewed opportunity to confirm that these smells were not coming from me or my body.

One morning after his breakfast, I was at the office when he picked me up. We were led by his nice cousin. We arrived at the laboratory. After checking in, we lined up and it was my turn. Vaginal and blood samples were taken. On the program were very detailed examinations of a long series of pathologies. It was after a few days that you had to come and take the results. These were satisfactory. I had nothing complicated, neither did my lap. I was very satisfied with it as the ultimate confirmation that I was doing the best, I was healthy, very healthy indeed.

Just like the previous treatment, I had to fill myself with eggs. Even though it was a bit too much for my genitalia because taken at such short notice, I chose to add them. Obsessed with where these smells came from, I wanted to end it even if that wasn't the solution. I had to stop those who sent them to me.

Soon after, the future husband left because the two families did not get along. The engagement date has been pushed back and there you go. So he left for another country, Germany where he lived and worked. He left me with the pictures, the smelly smells, the voices in my head. All interminable. I had these smells on my dishes, at the edge of my closet, on my veranda sometimes, in the hallways too.

Here are some pictures from this period:

Image: Before even seeing my boyfriend who I was to marry with, they sent him to me in my sleep. We were at a

<u>My brain attack by Miss TCHEUKO TCHAPDA MALVINA PRUDENCE.</u>

reception, it was pretty festive and everyone was having fun. I saw him, he was walking, talking, smiling.

Image: Pictures of me wearing my own pants, the pants I had put on two days ago to go out.

Image: Once in my sleep I saw the white sky opening up, out of that sky came out a yellow butterfly flapping its wings. I remember after I woke up from my sleep I got scared and walked down the street to the tar. I was still looking for cars to save myself. I opened car doors, finding nothing and no one, I went back to my room at home and fell asleep.

Image: Friends again I saw them in my sleep singing around a table.

Then my hierarchy at work decided to change my agency. I admit I asked permission not to go because I suspected I was seeing other people, other new people. I went so far as to talk to a professional elder, he reassured me that the goal was to enhance myself professionally. Despite that, I didn't see it well anyway. My survival depended on it.

It was one afternoon that I was told "Miss, you will go to Logpom" My complaint was not followed up and I found myself working in another agency.
When I arrived at this new agency, I was very well received with all the amenities and well installed. At the beginning it was mini training and coaching just to take over the job. It was pretty user-friendly, I liked it. But I was dented when I started to have them in my head. Almost everyone appeared on my nights. These new people were popping up in my brain, I didn't know what to do about it.

Image: Women at work giving me marriage advice.

Image: In my sleep, a glimpse of my old friends, more precisely my ex partners appeared to me at the same time. It was a well-edited visual that showcased their photos taken together. And there I confirmed that my life was within reach. My past experience had come out without me telling anyone. I admit it was very weird for me. Without telling my life to people I didn't know, they had as a story. How was this possible? Come to think of it, I was accusing someone who pirate into my brain. Even to this day I need clarification and precision on this matter.

Image: A friend and I by the water's edge, at the beach, wearing a white wedding dress. He wears me happy party style. Why such a scene? I do not know. What was the provenance according to you?

Image: Pictures of me in my own clothes, this frayed-down gold glitter mini dress adorned with a gold chain. They were sure they were spying on me, otherwise how could they have known this garment or seen me with it?

Image: I saw someone from my professional circle. I was with my father, we were visiting him in a not very clean neighborhood. While walking, we avoided the holes and ran away from being assaulted.

Image: At the back of a building there was a large courtyard. Downstairs was a door that gave access to the stairs. I went up and I saw people walking up and down these stairs. Then the scene ended.

These images overwhelmed my brain. I had lost sleep over it. There were nights when I barely slept. I had adopted the method of seeking sleep with my eyes open. It was very difficult. To this day these people who inserted me and who still do are known, have not been found, if not yet arrested.

In everyday life, we can denounce this by speaking of an infringement of human rights, if I am not mistaken, otherwise it will be necessary to seek legal qualification according to criminal law. But in my opinion, from this context, one should recognize the "right to sleep" to a human being.

At my new job, I led a still simple life: metro-work-sleep. But the recent ones were the nocturnal pictures, the bad smells and the feeling of being known. I was wondering how to get away from it all, I was thinking about euthanasia. I even went so far as to research it and later found I didn't meet the criteria. It seemed so

<u>My brain attack by Miss TCHEUKO TCHAPDA MALVINA PRUDENCE.</u>

huge to me that always wanting to run away from it all I attempted suicide. Following an injection of petroleum into my veins, I ended up in the hospital. The attempt was unsuccessful. At the hospital they cleaned my whole body, and once I got out I went to my father to spend my periods of convalescence. After some dressing sessions, I returned to work. I was going back to work again. The Lord did not allow these atrocities to take me away from him. It was clear, so I had to live and fight to stop it all. Images, smells continued. I was worried when one day I smelled much the same thing on another person around me. Then I concluded that the connection could be the business of several different people.

My job at the new agency was going pretty well. I was well evaluated and graded to the point where I was waiting for my contract. Weeks after the agency changed my place of work. We moved in and the work was going well. But strangely, I no longer smelled, the criminals were probably tired. Weeks later, management called me to terminate my contract. I was very sad about it, but he said he had to call me back.

So I was at home unemployed, impatiently awaiting the phone call that would put me back on work. The reappearance of the smells sent was that of basilic. As I used to cook with basilic. That day I was making tripe sauce and had omitted to put basilic in the condiments. I was lying in my bed then when the smell of basilic appeared in my nose. It was the ultimate confirmation that the scents had propelled me.
The demonstrations around me were unpleasantly picturesque, ranging from harassment to frustration, including extraordinary remarks and observations. I will tell you step by step how things unfolded.

People around me who talked about my own life, my acquaintances without prior discussion and without making an appointment, a sign that I was known. Suspicion that my head, my brain had been hacked. I was challenged by a device that I did not yet know how ...

Certainly it was known to everyone because just listening, I recognized the vocal tones of my old friends and entourage. Unless imitation, this certified their presence. But I never understood the reason for acting in secret, for looking at myself without bringing up the subject or even why not to have me safe immediately; since the question was already clearly defined.

The first remarks of this mess around me were when people around me called out the names of my old friends and boyfriends. All this without speaking to me directly. I observed this even at work, I was uncomfortable. Clues and words burst forth from everywhere, from all mouths. Then I made a link, links with my past life. Someone had narrated about my existence or what they knew about me and it had gone around, a whole round that got back to where it started, which was me. They talked about it so much around me, I wondered the reason for all this chatter in the workplace. Although I think it was meant to be good, I found this attitude a bit intrusive, out of context and not very helpful in my opinion. Faced with this I chose to keep my calm, believing that work occupied a preponderant place for me. I couldn't tell anyone about it because you can't share a private life with those who aren't in your private life circle. So I stayed focused on my job. My job that I loved very much.

Other surprising remarks were the ready-made, well-worded words that stood out from the rubbing of my clothes. The same when I fixed my bed or in the shower with the jets of water. The same thing when I scratched my ear, for example, I had messages reaching me most of the time telling me what was going on that I didn't see or didn't know.

Things got worse when I heard noises in my head. There was this possibility of speaking through a person's head or brain, and mine was subject to it. They took my head for a central transmitter or something. At the same moment of the images, I was subjected to audios from an unknown source but with the certainty that it was the initiative of men, human beings whom I will describe as malicious. It happened day and night, at work and after returning home. They used my head to be rude to other people. I listened to superiors and colleagues being insulted with bitterness and flippancy. I had the audios for my parents who were talking about enormities. We talked about their lives as well, their lives of which I didn't even know the story.

The stopper was pushed further when they attacked me too. This is when the company grants me access to the management software system used within the company. As we all know, that implies trust and recognized competence in the user. During this period a bizarre fact happened. When using the software, voices are endless. It was non-stop. Comments about people, family, superiors, and the inappropriate and rude nature of those comments.

At the same time, I had this feeling that friends and colleagues knew what I was going through, without telling me or asking me they had set up a system of marches. I believed in signals asking me to run away: car horns, the noises of neighbors (here I live in a mini city nicely painted in pink and green). Without understanding the meaning I started to walk when I heard a horn, hoping to find a car or a driver waiting for me to take me away from this mess. I believed in a discreet escape system set up by the protagonists concerned about my life situation and my brain exposed. I had to continue to live something concrete, which made more sense, especially my work. Both I worked and I followed these horn alerts. They insisted sometimes it looked like an injunction asking me to go out to walk, to look for them. To find cars to get in and hide in. I was thinking about that requisite of getting into a car and hiding and waiting for a driver to take me to safety. I had been asked to walk in my house on certain nights, sometimes at odd hours. I felt called upon during my work days and I devoted my break hours to them. But I had no results. So I chose to stay quiet, to devote myself to my professional work and to no longer give it importance.

Then I changed my place of work, I went to the other agency as you know. There it was the same scenario, the cerebral harassment continued. At work and at home. All around me was the same unease. Comments related to my past life, my entourage. The streets mingled with them, unless I was mistaken, I received actions, comments closely related to what I had experienced, my associates, my friendships. The smells continued. I was sorry when I first sniffed it on someone else: toilet smells.

My brain attack by Miss TCHEUKO TCHAPDA MALVINA PRUDENCE.

Apparently it wasn't just a person's business. Everything
suggested that we were facing an attack or even a tragedy
that could happen to anyone. In other words, everyone
could be subject to it. It was such a shame.
Faced with this, my father made me consult a priestess.
She prescribed prayers for me. To overcome these attacks,
I combined sessions of prayer and spiritual cleansing in
the name of Jesus Christ. Twice a week, after work I went
to the priestess to take care of myself and do my
purification sessions accompanied by prayers and
invocations. The goal was also to plead for divine
protection according to this boomerang I was facing.

Once I even worked a little later than usual, I stayed in
a room of the office, seeing that it was the end of the
day, the volume of the television was turned up. While
working I heard my name from outside, it was from TV. I
was very embarrassed, I admit. I did not understand the
reason for all this. Even less what it gave me. If there
was something to be done it would be done within the
standards and rules of the art, no need to call my name
everywhere. I continued to focus on my work. These noises
around me were very unpleasant, I didn't need them.
It was a big blow when the company ended my contract. But
I left with the assurance of being called back a few days
later. Something that I have waited three years in a row
without the expected effect. While I was waiting for this
phone call that would put me back in the business of
work, the martyrdom continued.

At one point I felt lonely, seeing the time and the
advancing age, I told myself that we could try something.
And considering the orchestrated damage on the planet. I
had a bad idea to get pregnant. So I went to the
hospital, to my trusted health center, to do tests and
take samples. Surely things happened behind my back and
before I came for a consultation. I was diagnosed and
removed vaginally. Knowing everything that was going on,
aware of the unusual situation we found ourselves in, I
chose to follow them by making this baby that way. I
trusted them. I thought he would show up in due course.
After the operation, I returned to do the exercises: lift
my legs up, tighten the vagina to store the semen, avoid
urinating to prevent leakage…. A few days later, I felt
nausea. They were repetitive. I felt heavy the following

days. Despite the complicated movement, I saw myself happy to live this first time: I had never been pregnant. But at the time I was on medication, and I was taking a product called "Prêle". I believe the latter has affected the pregnancy process. The proof is that the following month during my next period I saw a fetus come out of me. And I believe there were still fertilized eggs because the next month on my period I always extract formed eggs and other dishes. I felt very sad, I did not understand anything, but I got used to the idea because having consumed a product that I shouldn't.

As I raised above the songs that quoted me. They also spoke the others, the ones who had surrounded me. I was entitled to it all day long this time since I was at home now. I followed them through my neighborhood, the next door. The volume was so high that all the words that evoked the names of my acquaintances and I reached me crystal clear. I believe this neighbor was doing it on purpose. He repeated these songs dozens of times. I suffered of it when I was doing my housework, when cooking, during off-duty ... Once we argued to turn the volume down so as not to annoy the neighborhood. I would move away from it sometimes by going to sit outside to avoid these noises. Sometimes I would sit on a bench a little further and to the right of the building, since it gave way to the windows of the households, the music would always reach me. Sometimes at night people noticed my house and came by to play their music at such a high volume that the whole building was disturbed. I'm not sure how, but I made the connection with myself. I could not any more.

Considering the extent of the noise around my house, I also have to withdraw from time to time just to get a change of air and breathe a little. I was stressed to know that. You don't put someone in the spotlight that way. It was someone's initiative and I don't know who yet. So I used to take myself to a nearby hotel room in order to get away from it all a bit and recharge my batteries. Once settled into the bedroom with the desire to rest that I heard the names of my old friends on television, a suspicion that I had crossed borders. Sometimes I was in bed I heard famous voices speaking to me in the hallway. After opening the door to find out who

My brain attack by Miss TCHEUKO TCHAPDA MALVINA PRUDENCE.

it was, who might have a similar voice, I returned to the room not knowing what to do. I took rest, it was soothing away from the household and the noise.

This was not the case for the second time when I checked into a hotel room. This time, after paying and entering the premises, I was treated to the noise, to the songs in compilation playing at the back of the hotel. As I walked in I saw a married couple pass by, I guess it was the sound system related to that wedding. I had a not very pleasant stay there.

In the face of all this uproar, I chose to stay calm because I never expected that. I lead a rather discreet life, out of sight. If I am not wrong somebody said that to live happily, you have to live in hiden.

Obviously, undergoing the brainstorming, I called for help, just to tell my entourage, friends, family. I left emails, messages to friends, but their reactions were most surprising and disappointing. They remained without a word, without an answer, or a cough.

By thinking highly about it then I told myself that their voices, the car horns, were indicating me and I realized that they already knew it. They had chosen a way to make that was comfortable for them. I couldn't shake them any more.

When my lease ended I had to move out. Once downstairs, in my new house, there was less noise from the neighbor, no song. Even though those outside the barrier were playing it, it didn't go through my door much, my new door. I thought I was a sigh of relief, but to my surprise, I was treated to sounds and comments of an even more particular kind.

Here we are at the time of the expansion of the Corona Virus, of the Covid19. While prevention against the virus is in full swing, wearing a mask is an integral part of everyday life. All citizens concerned about their health preserved themselves.
This time it was words from my ex friends who would go out with my old friends. I believed in this possibility

since everything was known and it was already talking across borders. My phone contacts must have crossed paths already. Do we ever know. Otherwise why will I hear about them? I heard that my contacts had gathered and they were already going to famous people. They were moving through planes that landed in places not far from the neighborhood where I lived. The content of the rumors was that the authorities had already taken their place to settle the matter and that my hierarchy and friends were sitting down with them to jointly see the plausible solutions. There were rumors that movie actors were there to make a movie and identify local actors and travel with them. Also that there were religious representations present to get us out of this trap. And of course I, not knowing where these people were, I wisely expected to be contacted as I should. There were marriages with these foreigners. Weddings involving my family and where I was not invited.

Suddenly in my household, I noticed an actor's voice that I recognized and that I used to watch on M6. There was a weirdly enjoyable kind of exchange that we were planning to make into a movie screening, some kind of documentary. So given the grandiose and unique aspect of the situation I was going through, we felt it could be made into a feature film. It was a question of coming to seek me to start the realization of a movie.

To all these we say were associated images in my head, so I believed in their effectiveness. The rumors there were more than ever about my close person that I know. According to these reports, those persons had gathered for a solution to this case, something that I never touched.
The height, the unreal remark was the words coming from the animals. I had this surprising feeling that they were uttering voices and phrases.
As I was sitting on a rock outside the barrier of the building, around 6.30pm a female dog, black and white I believe, was walking past me all the time saying " follow me "," come "; "Follow me", "come", "follow me", "come", "she even hears?" He was looking at me as he walked along the path coming towards the main road he was still looking at me. Of course I couldn't answer or follow him, of course dogs and humans don't talk to each other; at

My brain attack by Miss TCHEUKO TCHAPDA MALVINA PRUDENCE.

least where I'm from it never happened except in the
movies on TV. That's how I sat and watched him walk away
until I couldn't see him anymore. Time to think about it,
time to reflect about it, I returned to my house at
around 8:15 p.m.

He looked like he was waiting for my moments of
relaxation because once again I come out another night to
sit outside, the same animal walks past me, this same
slender black and white colored dog walks past again me,
it emerged from him "follow me, come". I found him rather
handsome, used to seeing him when I sat down in the
evening, I already saw him as a pet of the moment. And I,
loving to laugh and appreciate, let out a burst of
laughter. But then I kept my mouth shut when this animal
said "she's laughing what eeehhh" Very surprised, I
looked at him until he left and walked away.
What analysis did I have of all this? It could be that
the reading of my brain phenomenon appeared so supra
unreal that even the animal species interfered in it;
either these had chips or microphones to warn me and
report me, until now I wonder from whom this initiative;
or then it was a trick of the evil one.
For information, it is 7:25 pm on 08/20 2021 at the time
of writing to you they make me smell foul odors for a
handful of seconds. Remember I don't see those who are
doing such a thing.

Another highlight was the people around me talking,
repeating and responding to me without seeing each other,
without having a conversation, and without phone, email,
or correspondence.

Can you please tell me where this has been observed
before? Me not at all in case. Noticed anywhere so far
this was the first time, never seen in the whole world. I
was in the middle of this phenomenon, I am the first
victim. Without wanting it, I was part of this "Never
been before"
The only assurance was that it was still common to
ordinary people. It was the initiative of men, human
beings who both wanted to invade and disturb but also who
were shielded from this act of delinquency.

My brain attack by Miss TCHEUKO TCHAPDA MALVINA PRUDENCE.

I suffered terribly from it. I never could bring myself
to it. I still suffer from it, they do it to me
everywhere I go: at home, at the office, at church, with
friends, at the wedding. This is how when I thought of
something, people would say it out loud to me. In my
house, for example, I wonder what I'm going to eat.
Outside I am told "you will not eat"; "You put too much
salt yesterday"; one day when i finish cooking outside i
hear "you have well prepared Malvinajeep ". Some would
say to me "Don't talk anymore". The days when I was a
little sick it was "Go to the hospital, take the
medicine"; or "make a child with your boyfriend" When I
walked people said to me "Go to this and that hotel,
they are there", some people said "don't work anymore".
Just as every time I read a sentence or a notebook, he
repeated to himself what I was reading.

I was also said like "This is exactly what you are
thinking about." Without opening my mouth to speak or
pronounce or say anything vocally. Because of reading my
ideas and thoughts through this instrument, this device.
It gives off a feeling of nervousness, astonishment
weird. I am upset to see the insulting and abnormal
aspect of the attitudes. We notice how things go against
the grain: we do not tell someone what he is thinking
without seeing it or conversing with it verbally. And the
expression is light.
Samely, I was hearing "We don't know you can imagine like
that" Until I saw this, I knew the stories and thoughts
shared only while discussing. And not by piercing the
skulls and brains.

In order to avoid this noise, I used to listen to music.
I also listened to him, taking a little air, sitting on
this rock where I saw this white and black dog. To have
moments of my own, I bought myself some headphones for
music; you know those mini devices with built-in memory
card. My dear music compilation was preventing me from
listening and hearing the noises and comments around me.
I refused to be invaded by comments about my past life,
that of my family, my friends. Passers-by, neighbors,
children all lent themselves to it. It bordered on
harassment especially since I need peace and it was not
my habit or context of daily life. They invaded me

because I had access to the contents of my head, my memories, my experience and by extension that of others who surrounded me in the past. I was listening to music, very beautiful melody. We all know its main characteristic, which is to soften morals. I had fun with the religious style, Cameroonian, American, English, Nigerian, Latin, French ... By dint of gaining a taste, I repeated and replayed my favorite songs in a loop, and to my surprise even in audio, I was passed messages, my name and that of the others I met.

It was very surprising and I was amazed. Here too I found that I had no respite. My life went around, it crossed borders.
In my new house, I kept walking, I scoured every nook and cranny of the neighborhood hoping to find a solution.
There was no difference between day and night to devote myself to it.
Same for the planes I expected. Because here began the intervention of the planes, but without mobilizing with ardor. The noises also started when I was living in the new house. Here I got wind that foreigners carried my knowledge with flying machines and that together they would work. Also I believed my family and workmates in relation with them for possible collaboration of films or others. I had pictures of them on TV sets, in make-up sessions, doing interviews… Then I came to the conclusion of the known **B,** probable future. Because I listened to these noises and believed them I got assaulted on a rainy night when voices asked me to run away and stop at the next car. Naively, I followed his directions that I heard through the walls of my house and had my bag of credit card and national ID card pulled out for me.

After that I doubled my effort, that didn't stop me from continuing to wait for help. Around me the rumors and gossip that said big brand owners came with opportunities to invest in the country. These took the opportunity to send for me by people who refused for what reason I do not know. Also, directors were there to make my friends into actors and find the talents of the country, castings would take place in hotels. Information that I have never been able to verify is why I am talking about gossip. Or it was either the known B.

My brain attack by Miss TCHEUKO TCHAPDA MALVINA PRUDENCE.

I lived in my new home for about two months and then my mom moved me out because of the financial difficulties I was going through, still not having a job at the time. When I got home I was put on pills. These tired my body. The goal was to rest but I didn't appreciate the effects on me. I needed to be in control of my body, to be in control. So I threw those tablets away. Shortly after, these came out of me. During this period I was entitled to incessant noise. Here I heard that the foreigners were present but I could not verify that, until today by the way. I was overwhelmed by the comments. According to these statements, foreigners and great personalities came to help me, they wanted to give me compensation. This one made me a billionaire. My friends and workmates received them and helped them have a good time in the country. It was after that I found out that these were comments on the **B** that it was possible to know.

Then refusing my mother's confinement, I escaped and had the idea to go to her friend's who was staying in a hotel in the city. He put me up and then we slept with his girlfriend on the same bed. Being in this room, I expected these personalities to reserve a room for me to wait for them, but none of that happened. But it wasn't long before I learned that she had called unsuccessfully. She was one of the ladies on the Forbes rankings. Then my mother picked me up from this hotel to take me home. It was a very disappointing night, having fled the confinements with nothing concrete in return.

For the second time I fled my mother's house, this time to my father's house. When I got home the welcome was cold at first, then the noises around the house did not help me. I continued to be the subject of chatter, but there were some who liked me based on what they saw of me in the past, present and future. But the noise was big, hard to bear. According to the statements, I had to walk to go to a stadium to wait for the planes which would come to carry me. I walked a lot to find these henchmen who were coming to my aid. I spent several days doing it, morning and evening. Those evenings when I saw the lights of the planes in the sky, all smiling and hoping for their eventual descent, I multiplied the hours of waiting. But those never came down. After the operation descent of the planes, I had the idea to receive the packages through their momentum coming from always high. Participants still had to use airplanes to do so. Even my entourage mobilized to throw something at me but no need to use the planes, they came by car and managed through the barrier or an orifice in the house.

The images were of a different nature. I was served the scenes that would take place: love scenes of people having sex. Others who fought against the bad guys. There were dinners in fancy places, friends walking the red carpet in Hollywood. They rubbed shoulders with the big Hollywood movie theaters and traveled by private jet. When I lived there it was very active: planes that wanted to descend, foreign voices, songs that spoke to me, the most spectacular scenarios, religious spiritual presence, research in hotels… As I said, I was told I was a billionaire and there was a consequent treatment to which I was entitled.

Because I continued to believe these horn signals, one evening I went out to explore the tracks in the neighborhood. I found a car, a Peugeot and then I went in and hid. I waited for hours lying in the back, then I heard someone knock on that car before I walked down a dark hallway. I went out but I couldn't follow him because it was too dark. Then I got into the next car, the rain had started. I thought someone would come get me, but none of that. Then my next car target was my father's, I went in there to hide and he was questioning when he saw this. I was telling myself whether or not I was talking about making me fly from this country or from the danger that was coming.

As it spread, Operation Rescue the Brained Victim, I suffered attacks from the blurry creature shadows sent to me. They invaded me and manifested their presence to scare me. And knowing that others saw what I saw, they were dissuaded, but others were not discouraged. By dint of prayer, these creature shadows disappeared. Come to think of it, it was mechanical manipulation on the part of those who were connecting me.

We had to work twice as hard. I went so far as to list the proposed solutions, organize and coordinate the operational aspect of the descents. It was long after that I knew it was a ploy to assess my management skills and abilities or my ability to organize my own rescue operation.

On the other hand, I have known kind shadows who came to encourage me, shadows in the faces of the people I saw on television. Some wanted to hear from me on specific issues, what was going on, what needed to be done to resolve the situation. Especially since the thoughts were read, the words heard. I was treated to let's say panoramic communication of people via shadows (really hard to describe but it's this description that seems closer to reality) Shadows through the walls of the bedroom, others to the sky. It was becoming a way of communicating nothing bad, I'll admit. I just don't think any of them were trying to get closer without being able to contact me normally. Besides, I never understood why until this day I had never been contacted feeling that he was known to all that I was going through. But anyway, we put that under the account of patience, things can arise at the appropriate time.

Image: Ants walking in rows, they formed rows of six. When I woke up I got chills, it took me three days to get rid of it.

Image: As I sought sleep, I saw the heads of people scrolling past, people I did not know from Adam or Eve. Here I had this unfortunate feeling that my brain was in the hands of several people this time around. And everyone had fun showing them all the photos they wanted, such as a son, a cousin, an aunt, a grandfather, a niece, a friend, a market vendor, ac child…. And there you have it, I was no longer alone living my nightmare.

Image: They were making montages of me walking into a reception, a room filled with white diners. It was a high class, bourgeois style reception. When I walked in, I noticed a friend sitting around a table talking to other people; then I went to sit on a chair not far from theirs. A few minutes later, I get up and walk towards an elevator with a glass of champagne in my hand without really knowing the reason for this trip. So the video ended and I woke up from my sleep. What did this video mean? I remain unanswered.

Image: In a room under construction, people surrounded and I was one of them. Then I escaped the circle and went up the stairs and hid. People were trying to catch up with me but to no avail. Soon after, everyone was gone.

Image: I was lying tired or sick, I don't know why, especially since these scenes do not give the reasons for things. So while lying down, an old man came to threaten me with a sword. Then another younger one came to stop the old man from harming me. This younger man seemed to care about me, to care about me and everything that happened to me.

The noises continued, some people trying to relate what they saw in their machine.

Around me I was silenced by my family and my acquaintances and friends, not to mention the physical abuse of my father. This one understood everything but choose not to support me. Every time I spoke to him about the presence of the organizations there, he scolded me like a child, thus filling the air. I was alone with this problem, except the shadow men who helped me in their own way. After beating me, which took me to the hospital, my father threw my suitcases outside his house. This is how I moved to find myself at my mother's once again. Once we got to my mom's house, a beating mom who struggles to feed us from the top of her three-step building. Having returned home, I was treated to the same pattern, that is, this communication in the shadows, people talking to you without a word, making gestures that think they can send you a message.

So before moving there again, I had negotiated to reassure myself that the lockdowns would not continue. I took my house keys. This is how I was free to move around. But the henchmen were gone. I took the opportunity to rest. The bad news is that the noises didn't stop. I was always watched, and everything I did and did was commented on. I was unemployed and started to

My brain attack by Miss TCHEUKO TCHAPDA MALVINA PRUDENCE.

apply. In that stride I got almost two full-time jobs that didn't last. Known to all, the sounds continued at work and at home. I started following the familiar voices again without seeing them and they didn't pick up the phones. I needed them to help me find a job, or give me a hand financially. I had to come to terms with it until I didn't call them anymore.

The first job I was in a call center I spent almost three weeks there I had to leave it because of the distance and the dangerous and inconvenient means of transport. I left him for the second job which only lasted a month, it was a probationary contract. Even here I was not at ease, it was unrelenting. Noise, inappropriate words, insults, rudeness constantly leaving the house to my place of duty and from the place of duty to the house in the evening. From bedtime to daybreak, throughout this cycle I was subjected to noise. Without forgetting the images which reached me in an updated way and according to the new faces that I met.

Image: During my nights, I saw my boss driving his car, his big car.

Image: As I slept, I saw workmates who walked with animal legs up the stairs. It was the stairs to my office.

Image: When I woke up, I remember that at night I was sent the head of the office colleague, he had his hands folded as when you want to ask for forgiveness. I admit I did not understand the reason for sending me these images of my new workmates.

In this company I spent a month. Then with the structure we separated and I resumed the path of the search for employment. I multiplied the interviews.

Image: I was invited to an interview at a company in the city. The ladies were talking to me for the position of Customer Advisor. There was another lady, an employee sitting behind me at work. I noticed her because she was a bit stout and dark. After this interview, I returned home. That same night, I had this lady sitting behind me who appeared in my brain. They transmitted this image of this rather corpulent lady in my brain when I slept. When I woke up it was "fleshy"

Another intolerable act was pushing my urine out. Having connected me to an electronic device, they succeeded, these criminals. Every morning I got up with urine pushed out, I was forced to squeeze my genitalia, adopting the Quigley practice. It is very annoying to know that something touches you or has access to your organ, to your bladder to the point of wanting to extract its contents without your consent or your need. And again, my body's normal process doesn't even require it. Without my permission, without knowing me, without seeing him, someone had access to my genitalia. It was intolerable.

This attitude of pushing urine out was repeated even on the way to the office. I was even a subject when I was making photocopies of my curriculum and my national identity card. I was looking for a job during this time. You know you have to work to live and I like working. It uplifts me a lot and I like to be useful. After paying the bill for the said photocopies, suddenly I feel urine asking to go out without even notifying me, as is often the case. I held them back in vain, squirming in all directions, wiggling my pelvis to avoid pissing on myself. As I walked towards the taxi parking lot, as I walked through the Coaf bakery, a few drops of urine came through and I felt wet. What uneasiness! I hoped I wouldn't get stained when I sat in the cab I took. Luckily my skirt didn't have a urine stain, I noticed it when I got home.

It went further when I saw that these gestures could pass through your body and be transcribed into you. That is, someone makes a gesture being miles away, this through you and you are experiencing it without any intention of making it. I will call them "introduced gestures and movements." I was the victim of rudeness and disrespect in the sense that these introduced gestures distorted my precepts and habits because they were of a very rude and disrespectful nature. This is how I was entitled to kicks, slapping hands (which slapped others) Through the introduced gestures, people used them to disrespect others in me. Associating with it. This is what I call myself a victim. Everything made me uncomfortable because I got involved in things that were not within my purview or my habits. Striving for perfection appears to me as a chosen guide to life. So doing well is for me like a message, a reference, a proposal from the Lord; doing well is a model leading to good results, peace of mind, trying to perfect and having good and beautiful manners can bring a smile to others. The bible tells us "love one another as I have loved you." "

Of course the physical abuse continued. Stinging sensations in certain parts of the body such as the legs, vagina, ribs, arms, nostrils, even eyes. They also pulled the nerves out of my brain.
By force of thinking about it, I realized that I had already been hacked for almost 2018. I believe yes, after a phone call from a friend, who answered one of my thoughts, I guessed that . I went to report it to a friend of my father but he did not follow up. I saw that there was a difference in my daily life: no noise or physical harm. I think that's what caused me to ignore it as the course of my life continued.

Until now I face the silence of my loved ones from everything that is going on, they just show up in the shadows and with their voices by the side of the road. As for the disorder following the connection, I do not understand why it continues. This questioning that displeases me and leads me to grasp and denounce. I want my brains all to myself and not within everyone's reach.

<u>**My brain attack by Miss TCHEUKO TCHAPDA MALVINA PRUDENCE.**</u>

THE CONTINUITY OF THE MOST RECENT IMAGES.

Even in my current writings I suffer from noise around my house, physical abuse and the hardest part my nights are still disturbed. Here is some evidence:

August 19, 2021. Today I am entitled to nudity images. As one can imagine it is very annoying to see scenes of people you know, moreover without having them nearby.
 I do not know what explanation to give for this, which is why other than an attack that is with conviction and rigor to denounce to the competent authorities. Several charges may arise from this attack or act. Those charges which, according to a simple reading, need to be updated or even contextualized by the texts and regulations. We can talk about brain torture, electronic abuse since it is through the electronic device. Can we also denounce espionage because we must have these nudities within reach in order to be able to introduce them into the brain of a human being when he is asleep. All contributing to the violation of human rights. The international organization in charge of the protection of human rights is also strongly and humbly called on this subject.

August 23, 2021: Someone walking with my pink underwear on their head. These boxers, I had washed them the day before. He had it on his head like wearing a coat and going to address a woman with .... When you wake up, when you think about it, it's incredibly creepy. Who could sleep with that kind of image in the night and in front of them. Clearly, this thug had to be stopped.

August 24, 2021: In my brain, the head of an Indian reaching me. He had on his head this crown specific to their culture. A kind of traditional tiara decorated in straw.

August 25, 2021: They introduced me to this image on the slide. I always see myself tied to a machine. Using an electronic or computer device, these criminals insert images into my brain when I sleep and even after sleep when I close my eyes.

<u>My brain attack by Miss TCHEUKO TCHAPDA MALVINA PRUDENCE.</u>

August 26, 2021: Today, when I woke up, my blush appeared to me. I have a pink one that I really like. I have no idea what this thug wanted with my blush.

The human being closes his eyes and associates your head or your image with some other image (may it be vulgar, sordid, monstrous, animal) and you see the scene in your eyes. We ask ourselves the question what would be the link authorizes and allows or will make this possible. What could be the nature of this link and its functionalities?

August 27, 2021: At my break, while I was resting with my eyes closed, I saw a Caucasian man walking with his friend both smiling and looking relaxed. Then suddenly, this man pulled down his pants and showed his shorts.

August 28, 2021: A wide, very wide mouth filled with big teeth.

August 29, 2021: A woman lifting her dress and showing her thigh.

- Feathers or hairs of an animal that want to leave on him and start to get down.
- Two roosters face to face.
- The scrolling screens, like a mouse manipulating electronic files and data.
- A man crossing the road and passing an ML car in front of him.
- A little girl with big braids looking at me, then she starts dancing for a short time.
- An grand mom stretching out her arms wide open and trying to dance.
- An insect that swivels on a table.

August 30, 2021: A man wearing heavy underpants and kneeling down looking forward.

August 31, 2021: A face without a smile but showing its little teeth not clean and all sharp.

September 1, 2021: Me driving a small car. Then another car resembling a Hummer. I drove it with difficulty since the pedals were foreign to me. And if I remember correctly, it caused a little accident.

September 2, 2021: I witnessed a scene where there was an opportunity for free visas. It was enough to deposit documents in a room to the right. The nature of the documents I ignored them. There were two of my old friends standing, I could see them standing one in front and the other behind. Everything suggests that they were coming to assist a young woman who was also applying for a visa. The latter was sitting on a sofa in a main room. In the video, I witnessed this scene and then it cut off.

September 3, 2021: That day when I woke up, I saw a man holding a woman's hand. She sent me kisses with a smile. They were white and very oddly enchanted.

I also saw a forearm embroidered with white thread. What could that mean? The unusual and uncommon aspect of this image was creepy.

September 4, 2021: Tonight comes to me an old friend, surrounded by other friends. I was one of them. Together we chatted. Everyone was speaking to the issue raised by one in the group. She wondered what to say to her father when she slept outside the house. The latter had looked for his daughter last night because she had dropped out. So each in turn would give a piece of advice, one of which was to send a message to his father to reassure him. Another tip was to tell her the truth.
Also that night, another excruciating image was sent to me. It was an open mouth exposing yellowish dentition. There were teeth placed on top of each other. Horrible picture.

September 5, 2021: Tonight there is a video of my window not closing. In real life it usually closes at both ends. And so in the video sent, the window had mesh to close like I do every night.
After a few hours that same night, I saw an offender waiting for me to open that the same window. Once I do them, he took the opportunity to throw something round in shape and not easy to identify. Then I woke up.

<u>My brain attack by Miss TCHEUKO TCHAPDA MALVINA PRUDENCE.</u>

A few hours later, I saw myself screaming because I saw
bandits on the top of the house gate. I was really
screaming out loud.
And when I woke up to check if these bandits were really
there, then this time I saw with open eyes a rooster or
hen on a rope flapping its wings to hold itself up and
not fall over it.
At daybreak, half an ear of corn is displayed in my head.

September 6, 2021: That day I saw myself giving birth to
a child who came out through the belly. Hyper weird. Then
I saw children, quite well. The smile that this image
could provide was not enough to subtract the anger I felt
from sending these images into my brain when I slept.

September 7, 2021: In the scene of this night, one of my
hierarchical superiors, and two of my old friends are
gathered. One of them spoke of him as a man to be taken
into marriage. He was a potential male for the couple and
a young girl was asked to cheat on him. In another room a
former friend who was struggling to get her boyfriend's
attention. I was as an intermediary where I advised the
latter to make efforts towards her and reassure her. Then
they made peace and agreed to get married at the end.

September 8, 2021: This night was the most bizarre of
all: a woman without a mouth or without lips if we can
put it that way. The part of the head where the mouth is
located was all black. She was very short but a little
chubby. Behind her was a monkey. My mother was sitting in
an armchair with her arms crossed. We were in a room
awaiting the start of hostilities, the nature of which I
do not know. This mouthless lady was forcibly holding my
hand to lead me into another room where there was a
newborn baby on a table. Next to it sat a man and a
woman. I know the layout of this room because we went
through it beforehand.

A few hours later that night, I saw messages following an
exchange on the phone. I received writings with uncommon
meanings and spellings.

September 9, 2021: Today I saw two bottles on a table. A
bottle of grenadine and another of beer. This image
attests to what I am seen in my private cubicle because I

My brain attack by Miss TCHEUKO TCHAPDA MALVINA PRUDENCE.

usually drink this cocktail mix (tango) because I like it.
These images that appear when I try to sleep and when I seek sleep. This shows the difficult side of the matter, the abuse suffered by the brains of a human being. This is all horrible! We wonder what the link is and where do these images come from or at least their inspiration?

September 10, 2021: When I wake up, I remember a shop selling clothes, more specifically jackets. Inside there was a lady standing. I asked her where the owner of the store was, and she told me he was away. Behind me came out a man, he presented me with some jackets, which I would say rather pretty and to my size and my bouquet.

September 11, 2021: Lying on a bed, there were people around me, one of them a TV series actor. Together we saw people fighting. Then some brawlers arrived in the room we were in. I lay face down after I got under the bed to escape these brawlers. Those who were around me I no longer saw in these images. Then I woke up.

September 12, 2021: This night was almost blurry, I slept with almost nothing on my mind, at least this morning I don't remember much.

September 13, 2021: I had an image parade that I don't really remember.

September 14, 2021: During the day, I closed my eyes, these criminals send me a pineapple head with feathers.

- A girl in a long, dirty dress hanging out to the ground.

- A man with the mouth without in mature.

On the night of September 14, it was very strange to voice a friend of a friend sitting around a table with his friends. Then having paced with my father, my brother and another young girl. We met them where they were, then took a table next door. We were in a sort of room made of wood, plank. After the friend joined us, he had a long chat with my father, exchanging smiles and the latter handed him money bills for a plantation business. Soon after another friend came and sat down on a chair in the plank room. With a smile on his face, he exchanged with the others. Then hop I woke up from my sleep.

September 15, 2021: That night I saw the living room door wide open in the middle of the night. When I got up to close it there was a rather dirty woman with a slightly fuzzy face coming down from our wall after climbing. But I managed to close the door anyway. So I go to my bedroom window, I see the same woman who wanted to open it. I shouted alert to the bandits as I opened both sides of the window. Then I woke up. It seems that this person is the same one who makes the noise around the houses of the citizens.

September 16, 2021: After a demonstration whose nature I do not know, I was with a group of girls. When they got out of there, they started to run. I, too, avoiding a woman who was making suggestions that didn't interest me, I started running. It was a question of going up a slope, which I did with my back turned towards the normal direction: in fact I went up the hill with my back turned. Then I ran up the hill to the place and the woman with the interesting proposals followed me. I ran at speed, afterwards I extended my strides to increase speed in the race. I was running towards the house, my mother's house. Then the race was done on the four limbs, very surprising. Then I was racing on my own two legs and got to the gate of the house and rang the bell. I'm talking about my mother's house because I currently live there and having the feeling of being watched, these criminals stage editors already know my routes and use them to insert them into my head.

October 5, 2021: Two chicks, one pivoting back on itself. A house that a white man had bought to house people. This man wore a wedding ring. The next day hand, this house was occupied by a woman who occupied one room, and the other room was occupied by a man. It was much more of a rented suite for a meeting. Then I woke up and remember the walls weren't very clean. In the room occupied by this woman there were so many people. Then I visited her when I saw that she was surrounded by her father and her sisters, all seated on sofas glued to the different walls.

<u>**My brain attack by Miss TCHEUKO TCHAPDA MALVINA PRUDENCE.**</u>

October 6, 2021: A very oddly shaped man hanging from a tree. This man was walking away from his tree to approach me. I had all of this in pictures when I closed my eyes.

October 7, 2021: There was a friend, an acquaintance who created talks with her friends. They took turns complaining to us. We were a group of people: one man, two girls and this young lady who had problems with each of her boyfriends she dated. Also, very horrible was the image of the tape, the plaster I had that covered a wound on my arm.
This adhesive plaster, I tried to remove it little by little, logically feeling a big pain.
Also on the night of October 7, there is a helicopter flying at high speed. In short, the normal look worthy of a machine of this type. So the latter passed and he brought out a wad of banknotes which had fallen on the balcony where I was. This scene was very illustrative of my situation, it was proof of what my wishes were heard and noticeable. They knew that I had expressed the need for a helicopter, it could fail to come down and carry me, throw me a package which would reach me and be within my reach. This is what the scene in my night conveyed: they wanted it just as much as I did.

October 12, 2021: Me taking customer orders in a bar. To my left was a girl who wanted me to take orders from other people but I was resentful.
October 13, 2021: Two people: a man and woman about to kiss each other.
October 14, 2021: Two men sitting in an office. And I was going back and forth to surely manage a number of things. I say surely because these scenes do not give details as to the reasons and motives for the actions.

<u>My brain attack by Miss TCHEUKO TCHAPDA MALVINA PRUDENCE.</u>

THE DIFFICULTIES SHE HAD TO FACE.

The complications encountered and suffered throughout are multiple. We bring them out so that the seriousness of the situation is measured and the penalties incurred take place. The authors must take responsibility for their actions if not repair their wrong.

The images that came to me asleep kept me awake, attributing a troubled sleep to me. For almost 3 years I have never had a peaceful sleep. Devoid of normal nights, how easy would it be for a human being to get through the day? These monstrous, scary, horrific pics made me very pissed off and angry.

In the early days, I understood these attacks very badly. I thought they were periodical, I told myself that they would have an end. I had given it a time limit before I could leave them, in other words I had planned to leave this life so as not to see them again. Nights spent, I continued to suffer the ugly so I went to the pharmacy to buy a syringe and a liter of petroleum from a street vendor. Seeing that the atrocities of images did not stop, I put on sexy clothes, white lingerie, in a hurry to be done with these images. Lying on my bed, with the petroleum-filled syringe held in my right hand, I targeted a vein with the other hand, I introduced the liquid into that vein. Then my chest started to beat strongly. I drew strength into the same process on my right hand this time, but I couldn't. So I waited for the liquid to work in my body. The mixture with my organs gave me palpitations of the heart, the scent of oils coming out of my nostrils and my mouth and a general weakening. I had written a kind of will in which I left my savings to my little brothers and sisters. I wrote it by message to my big brother. Shortly after, he called me to understand. He asked me a whole bunch of questions and found me in my household. He was accompanied by my two twin sisters.

My brain attack by Miss TCHEUKO TCHAPDA MALVINA PRUDENCE.

I hadn't made it, the liquid didn't have an immediate
effect. My sisters and my brother helped me to take a
taxi, together we went to a hospital where I was
completely cleaned of this toxic fluid in my body. My
days in this place consisted of intravenous and rest.
Then my hand had surgery that was very painful when I
woke up from the anesthesia. Added to that was the stress
of paying the bills because my father was reluctant to
take care of it…. I spent almost two weeks in this
hospital. I was wrong. But I made a point: the footage
ceased for almost two days without reappearing. The days
after they resumed. And I got back to work and the life
of cerebral harassment that was now mine. After work, I
had to go to the hospital for cleaning and bandaging the
wound. I went back there until my oil-injected hand
healed. The back and forths in total are ten sessions,
especially since I went there almost twice a week.

The endless nature of the image and video insertions
makes me tired, morally exhausted. Every night I am a
victim of it. The limits are exceeded when human rights
are violated. Imagine the horrific images endured at
night and shared by a number of people as a result of my
life and connected head. Once the inhuman night has
passed, you have to face the day. This day which is now
made of the noises of the invaders, the shadows of the
people who wish to send you messages, of those who seek
the argument, of those who know you are connected and who
do not speak to you, of those who take still have time to
write or call you. After weird nights and sleeps, you had
to manage these days, do it this way.

My known hacked head, my abominable manipulated nights
left me perplexed at the start. I initiated the dialogue
to find a solution but to no avail. The night I was
staying in my own sleep, I was a spectator, we were all
there because they were there to watch me go through it
without saying a word or doing anything about it. The
fright at these monstrous and far-from-ordinary images
was enormous. At work, as a family, you had to look in
their eyes for a little compassion, but nothing. Through
their eyes, I wanted to have their opinion, their
analysis, their appreciation. There emerged a little
disgust, uneasiness. Attitudes also gave me answers. Some
were nice but others weren't. The indisposition towards

<u>My brain attack by Miss TCHEUKO TCHAPDA MALVINA PRUDENCE.</u>

people I knew at work and at home was great. Without being at fault, I cared, wondering why I have to see them in sleep? Why were we tied this way? It was difficult to move forward like this, but it had to be. The course of things, of life naturally prevailed, although it had become unusual.

We had to deal with the sadness because of those who lived my brain hacked and invaded at night and who did not want to talk to me or pick up a phone call. They had no doubt adopted the position they liked, but the feelings and consequences are no less unacceptable. Having my brains accessible, I must have gone through attempts to destroy it. Some people gave me the injections just to make me dementia. They blow me through the skull invoking witchcraft. With all kinds of objects they tried to hurt my sweet little brain. Every night I got angry with those who touched my brain, forcing them not to do it anymore. It was my brain after all, I was the main owner.

I was also undergoing in my head my hacked thoughts and the people who were using them. Of all ages we know that this is not a normal way of life. So imagine the frustration of knowing that line was crossed. I was confused, overwhelmed. To be subject to it appears to be a very bad turn in life, in my life. That's all I don't live normally anymore. This is how there were some that stole my thoughts, my ideas or were inspired by them. There was this possibility of stealing my future plans and I was not reassured. There is an insecurity emerging. I had to shout, scream, repeat several times not to connect my head or my brain. Alerting every day was not easy.

Carrying a head of read and exploited thoughts to disturb me was nothing human. I felt it was like a machine carrying databases to keep and do everything to prevent information leakage. Sometimes I was disturbed to send my brain requests for information. Those around me wanted me to remember past stories to read them in my brain. I found it very annoying and rude. People would say one or two words and phrases related to my buried stories, the goal was for me to remember it so that they would have the information clearly. They had made it a daily habit

<u>My brain attack by Miss TCHEUKO TCHAPDA MALVINA PRUDENCE.</u>

to have fun conjuring up memories near me, I will put it that way. They played where it was not allowed, the context and the environment did not allow it. I cried about it. I had to ignore the attacking remarks, try to focus on something else and things that are more important like my daily life at the ready second and minute.

When I got home, I was green. I resented people for disturbing me when all I wanted was to stay focused on my normal life. I was getting angry throwing away the gifts, shoes, cups and screaming of overload, and invasion as I saw the relay in the vicinity of my household. Neighbors also had a habit of playing with the words memories. I remember one afternoon, I was passing an alley, I was looking for cars to help me again. A group of people probably students because they were seated near the university campus; one of these people I did not know uttered a sentence at the same time as the one that was being said in my head, very indignant, I came home and had a fit, I was very close to the consumption of toxic liquid for the second time. I cried all the tears in my body.

My head was in constant pain, it became very embarrassing when even without sleeping people sent me who loved each other. Pictures of people I knew having sex. The scenes in all their details: from penetrations to hugs to moans.

Sometimes in the evening, I looked at the sky, admiring its different colors: red, white, blue. I wondered when it would end and at the same time I was arming myself with the courage to hold on.

Several evenings, through the walls of my household I could hear sighs. Those nights, I think it was also the voice of someone I knew. It was another way of attacking me, without really knowing why. I had to accept their refusal to use the discussion leading to a solution. There was a bit of childishness and vulgarity I think. What kind of individual could choose to approach a woman's household and display her antics in audio? You had to lack maturity somewhere.

My brain attack by Miss TCHEUKO TCHAPDA MALVINA PRUDENCE.

I was annoyed when I saw old comrades strutting around with the strangers. They had made the trip and were supposed to come for me. In hotels, they ended up with my friends who were also supposed to help me. I saw the mixes in mating. Women who had fun with all types of men. And men who got into the bodies of a lot of women. The hardest part was that were concerned my friends, my brothers and sisters, my fathers and mothers, my acquaintances and those who just heard about…. There were scenes of weddings, dinners, parties where guests danced, city tours, meetings, negotiations to pick me up, even arguments. I was disappointed because they had sidelined me supposedly because I was not ready and they were negotiating who would marry me.

As bizarre as it was, I must have experienced the apparent silence around me, yet they were aware of everything that was going on. Learning that they had chosen to pair up, although after some thought these were ready-made stories. Living this silence was sad. She had been waiting for a long time for someone to come and talk to me clearly and in due form. I needed it because I was looking for a solution.
Finally, it turns out that these images were the digest of what would happen, of **B** in other words. Or it was the interplay of interventions made with the imaginations of each one. I don't know how people accessed it or how it got to my head, to my eyes, but they demoralized me, causing me nervousness, heartache, grief and disappointment. All kinds of images combined with noise bothered me.

The noises were making in my head. Someone who talks in my head like it's a microphone. There were some who said things that were not pleasant at all. Sayings like "We're not here to joke"; "We are serials killer" At first glance these words seemed to relate to the attitudes of adolescents or dangerous and childish delinquents. They were rude when they ate in my ears, farted there, made me smell their foul odor from their bodies, from their smelly mouths, from their dirty pools, from their shoes and feet. They put my face in contact with their evil and delinquent acts and intentions, devoid of social and Christian values. I was so annoyed, not falling into the category of my dating, I only saw them as perpetrators to

My brain attack by Miss TCHEUKO TCHAPDA MALVINA PRUDENCE.

be punished. They were to be reprimanded for the common good, for peace and quiet in the homes of honest citizens.

The noises around my household, the lack of peace and quiet wherever I went. At church, during my prayers, at home where peace and quiet should reign, at my mother's, at my father's, at the hotel I used to escape the noise, at the ice cream shop, during demonstrations, during receptions, in the taxi too it was the shit of the inconvenience. I could not any more. Sometimes, during their meeting, the neighbors would chant my name in their house. We cannot be invaded in this way especially by people we do not know and without direct contact with. Some comments were offensive, hence the inconvenience. From these noises came the gestural comments of the shadow men. Hearing of the participation of the good guys, the bad guys came out to imitate and act badly. There were interventions in the shadows that only did harm and provoke a quarrel. It was so nauseous to know that adults could indulge in such low behavior. These offenses also had to be managed in the shadows. They had to be pushed aside, pushed back as best as possible because they had no right to approach me like that, nor to break into my house with bad manners or questions; having nothing to prove or explain to them as I was at home without harming anyone, not having connected anyone or extending any invitation. It was about putting an end to it and avoiding this improper reflex. Screaming and shouting were the cues because I didn't admit that to me.

I will not fail to bring up the fact that these noises generated the steps to try to escape. Tireness of the legs and of the mind, vain efforts, ridicule, unanswered questioning and aggression were the results of these walks. As I entered the cars, I believed in signals from people who wanted to help me. I may be wrong. I felt obliged every time I heard an insistent horn.

I paced open the doors of cars whose owners I didn't know. I took risks going into the open ones. I imagined explanations to give to the owners of these cars when they found me there. Once I was driven, thinking I had reached the end of the process, but the drivers drove me home. Another time I waited in a car all night until the early hours of the morning, at the sound of the rooster, not seeing anyone, I went home to sleep. Several other nights, when I was going out, I would make long roads crisscrossing the whole neighborhood and then I saw people I seemed to know, I called their names to be sure but only received silence. I would receive some sort of instruction from familiar voices and act on them. I packed my bags to walk and search. The hardest part was hearing the known voices even on the way and not being able to see them or have any precision as to what to do. Sometimes those instructions would take me to hotels to find out who might be waiting for me; you had to ask for a friend at reception, find out about a reservation on behalf of my own family, and even quote the names of my father's friends. Because at one point it felt like everyone was already together, involved, and wanted to hide, so the only thing missing was me. So without even understanding, I had to obey the instructions that came to me either from a wall or from the top of my house roof. In view of the seemingly critical situation, I continued to seek solutions from the cars. To the point where at each exit, a stroll, a visit from the priest, at Mom's office, I lent myself to the approach of getting into the cars. By this time I had moved to the bottom. During this operation of the walks, I was determined to speak to people I did not know, passers-by who wondered about my repeated presence in certain places.

Once, these instructions took me round the hotels. From taxi to taxi I searched for my family and friends at these hotels. It was in the evening when on my way home I stopped in a building owned by my Russian friends, where they were staying. On entering this building, I found no one. I took the stairs looking from door to door if I could find my Russian friends especially since I had forgotten their door number. So I waited at the stairs, I remember I spent the night there. I slept on the stairs of a building, I had never done that. Then the sounds of a helicopter, so I climbed up but couldn't recover. I returned to the stairs. I also expected people to come and get me to escort me, but none of that. Then the receptionist finally came out and asked me a series of questions. I must have done so much comedy for him to agree to give me a free night's room. But the one he offered me was not habitable, I had to get out. This front desk attendant was kind when he paid my taxi bill. Because once I entered the building, I didn't come out even to pay the taxi bill. So the taxi driver came back to claim his money, and the building receptionist helped me return it to him. I waited for help until morning had risen and I went home, still sad.

And I have attached importance to these instructions at all times, even at odd hours. It caused me to be assaulted around midnight. After hearing from the top of my house that my account had been replenished, that the family was going on a trip and therefore I had to stay and make do with this money. To get away, I had to go to a car at that time indicated above, I slowly executed. No sooner said than done. When it was time to go out, there was a power cut but not so important to prevent me from going out. I walked through the door with a big and small bag, I put the key towards the window. Then I went through the barrier, I think I saw some headlight sets and I went in that direction. It was raining little drops. I walked calmly to this car and put in a timeout. A few seconds later a motorbike came towards me and an individual climbed down with knife in hand. Further I followed a voice "cuts" and the bandit cut my little bag. I screamed alerting the neighborhood. I saw them take away my credit cards, my ID, my so cute bag, and the jewelry it contained. The rain was increasing. I came home with the big bag. While entering my house, the rain had flooded the room, the shower and the living room, so the power did not come back. A first had just happened to me, I couldn't believe it. So exhausted I slept on my bed with the water left on the floor. It wasn't until the next morning that I was able to get the water out of the ground. The next day I had a visit from my mother as I had informed her of my assault. I was so sad about it. What a complicated turn. I think I did at least eighty laps looking for cars with a million steps.

I couldn't spare you the long hours of waiting by the roadside when the plane was to pick me up. I struggled with rainy, very early morning and other late night expectations. Thinking about it, I remain nostalgic because the planes came very early and very late to pick me up, but my availability was limited due to the fact that I did not live at home and had to submit to the curfew of my father's house.

During a year, I made I believe about fifteen visits to the banks to go and withdraw the pennies that I had supposedly been deposited. What desolation! Far from being obvious I had to go there to check every bank comment. I always lowered my arms when the cashier replied "Madam, your account is empty"

By dint of walking, I thought I would improve the idea by waiting for them at my house, in my surroundings instead of going away from the house. The complications continued. The fictitious or electronic but visible animals that wanted to approach me. Once I spent the night under the stars waiting for someone to come and pick me up. I knew my friends were already mobilized, I heard that they came to pick up those concerned near their house. So I waited until tonight for them to come and pick me up like the others. I was sitting on a bench outside my door behind me there was a big rooster trying to approach me. He looked electrified. Three times he tried to approach and then disappeared. It was cold but I kept waiting for someone to come and rescue me. I slept on the chair. I would wake up each time with my head tilting down from the lack of a pillow.

One night again I got scared when I saw a man spiraling through me at lightning speed to enter a door behind me. I was still waiting for help, standing in front of my own door. I spent almost two hours standing there just to be ready to run to the sound of a vehicle horn; then I sat down.

The attacks became more pervasive when I started to see the bad representations as well, the evil attacks. Here I lived with my father, at bedtime I could see animal shadows.

I also had the idea to toss the pennies at home or write me a letter or drop me an envelope. I waited hours outside on my verandas because these operations took place at my house, my mother's house and my father's

My brain attack by Miss TCHEUKO TCHAPDA MALVINA PRUDENCE.

house. I wasn't too comfortable with having to do the
same thing everywhere when you just had to maximize.
Day and night we were always spectators of the disorder
following the noise and physical abuse that still had to
be endured.
I felt my body being electronically beaten, pricked,
stretched, it was painful. It all started as soon as I
arrived at my father's, it's been a year and a few
months. Every day I have the body that we hit, the organs
that we stretch, the shoulders that we push, bites in all
parts of my body. We are September 08, an individual
injected me with a substance by this route in my head, my
brain since September 07, that day I felt a very strong
pain on the left side of my head . The effects are
disastrous. I feel stings all over my body and it doesn't
stop. Similar effects have been manifesting for two days.
I undergo them to the head, eyes, forehead, nose, back,
chest, shoulders, ribs, elbows, thighs, knees, legs,
toes. Through his shadow, he came to insult and threaten
me. I had proof that it was the result of the bad
intentions of an individual with criminal tendencies.

These bodily break-ins continued when I returned to my
mother's house and until today they do not end. People
who blow my back, on my face. There were strange
sensations on my skin, these were repeated and I had to
cover my face so as not to feel them. I suffered various
kinds of abuse. You had to wrap your head to sleep so
that you would not insert an object or an animal through
this device. For instance, It is October 18, 2021, I am
currently suffering from pain in this left part of my
brain from my nostrils. Because this criminal created a
hole in my head. since almost ten days he has introduced
an object into my head via this device, and he punctures
gradually which has generated a kind of pit which is seen
to be too painful.
 He had this ability to grab a strange creature on its
back. Many times I went through this and ran into the
incense fire to burn it. Sometimes when she gripped like
that, all I had to do was turn around and the spiritual
force that was at our side would react.
Still in my body, I experienced burns, heaters. There
were times when I walked like I had no bones in my body.
My legs and arms took a hell of a beating. At times I

<u>My brain attack by Miss TCHEUKO TCHAPDA MALVINA PRUDENCE.</u>

felt them empty. I was just wearing a membrane with no content. It was new and very scary.
One day I got up and felt empty of the parts that house the ovaries. I alerted everyone around me by message. I told my mom about it, and got mad at her when she hesitated to take me to the hospital for an x-ray. I yelled in the car because she wanted to take what I was saying lightly. A few days later, very worried, I finally had an x-ray. And everything was there.

The smells propelled over my parts and around me were demoralizing. I had to arm myself with a lot of courage and self-confidence to move on, get up in the morning and keep working. It was with big, disturbing curiosities that I checked my lingerie in the bathroom. With each propelled smell, I would run into the toilet for an inspection of my pelvis. I was tired of it.

In addition to my long list of setbacks, there is an attempted forcible confinement. Because I explained to him the strange situations I was going through. She brought me prayers and a visit to a religious caregiver as a solution. We went once to this healer who would give me satisfaction. My mother took me to this lady. This place was not very clean and there was a corner, I noticed candles there. There was also a mother lying with a child, a young girl in the kitchen, and two fellows. After long minutes of waiting, I wanted to leave. My mother didn't want to. This is how I took the road back when these two fellows followed me. I did not want to answer them, I did not have a good idea of them. Then they pulled my hand to bring me back. He made me sit down and wait. Against my will ? I didn't accept that. I felt in danger from this kind of negative animosity so I looked at his electricity meter insistently and in detail so that he could be spotted. I held on to a pole to keep from moving forward. There was a gutter that led out of the perimeter of this house. When I tried to cross, the fellows would prevent me. I went back to hold the post; I did it until the lady came by motorbike. Once I got there, I stood on this pole, she surrounded me with salt, she threw an egg in my face and then sprayed me with jets of water that she had previously salted.

My brain attack by Miss TCHEUKO TCHAPDA MALVINA PRUDENCE.

She threw me salt, she broke the eggs on my forehead. I told her I didn't want this treatment. She insisted, asking me to go to that melted candle room. I was reluctant and the fellows carried me to get me there. Once inside, she asked me to undress, hardly I did. Along with another lady, they hit me with the Peace Tree and I confirmed that it was no longer about healing. They hit me and it was very painful. Then when she gave me a lick powder I refused, that's when she called the guys to come and force me to do it. They hit the ground, dragged me through the wet sand to force me to drink a liquid as well. I shouted with all my soul, I invoked the holy sacrament. Then they pulled me to the ground, made me lay my head back, they tried to put the liquid in my nose. I think they wanted to suffocate me so they twisted me left and right to keep them from touching my nostrils. It didn't look like an attempt to heal anymore. I screamed out loud, then they left me, lifted me up again offering me this black powder to lick. When I pretended to lick it, they put me through the same physical torture. It wasn't the same when I heard a man talk about a million, the grandmother said she wanted four million. Then she started to dance, turned her pelvis. I shouted out with all my might calling on the holy spirit for help, asking for my mother's help. They wanted to suffocate me with water, and that powder.

I was so out of breath. THANKS TO THE LORD they let me out. Sometime later they went to buy a drink, each holding a beer in their hand. They even offered my mom a beer. I was sitting all injured and covered in bits and sand, my mother took a picture of me. The unkind grandmother would ask me to wait in another room, which I refused. Then they asked me to leave. I saw a new man coming and then I ran away from that place. I stopped transportation to get home, no one carried me. Then my mother got in the car and I got in and she drove me to my house. It was a very big mishap for me. I regretted it bitterly.

The insertion of the pictures and the physical abuse had deceived everyone. My family when they heard about what I was going through chose to tell me about it with not-so-helpful medical consultations. In hospitals they believed in schizophrenia and in the need to fall asleep to avoid

<u>My brain attack by Miss TCHEUKO TCHAPDA MALVINA PRUDENCE.</u>

the noise of criminals. I got clinical injections and
unnecessary tablets. It all started with my father who
took me to a hospital for schizophrenia where they gave
me pills. These have completely dispossessed me of my
body. I no longer had any physical strength and was
completely delusional. I had to put those pills aside
because work was going back to normal. And as soon as I
did not drink them, my father hit me like a kid without
however understanding what I was going through. It was
not a beautiful impression. That day he hit me for the
first of two blows on the buttocks because of a
misunderstanding.

A year later, still in this hacked brain movement and
chatter around me, I was trapped by my mother, she wanted
to force me into this same hospital. She picked me up
from my house for a so-called ride. She rolled and rolled
again when suddenly I noticed her way to this hospital. I
got out of the car forcibly. While trying to take the way
home, the police detained me. They had checked my papers
and then made me sit in their cabin. A few minutes later
they wanted me to go with my mother in her car, which I
refused. They forced me and then I accepted so as not to
be subjected to violence, they were armed with sticks.
Once in the car, to my surprise, two men got in with me;
one on the left and one on the right. I felt insecure
because one was dressed as a police officer and the other
was not. I had this feeling that she was going in a
different direction because she wanted to cross the road
to the hospital and a man in yellow came to stop them. We
got out of the car to enter the hospital. These two men
were still following us very strangely. The man in yellow
made me sit in a chair opposite a doctor's door. Damn,
the guy who wasn't in cop clothes sat down next to me.
Either he was coming to watch me or he was mean, anyway I
don't know what he wanted with this guy. I wanted to run
away from this place because I sensed something that I
wouldn't like.

A few minutes later I entered this office room and closed
the door. Then I went to another room on the right, here
there was a bed. I tried to close it but the lock was
broken. And the man in yellow entered. Caught up in a
comedy, I pretended to want to urinate and defecate, so
he went and got me a mobile pissoir instead of leading me

My brain attack by Miss TCHEUKO TCHAPDA MALVINA PRUDENCE.

to the bathroom. I understood that it would be difficult
for me. Suddenly this gentleman entered the room with a
lady who was holding a tray in her hand. I thought he
would hurt me. That's how he pinned me to the bed, turned
my arms back, and the lady gave me an injection. When the
man in yellow left me, I was wet with urine and my arm
ached. Finally we left this hospital, the two men were
still following us and entered the car with us. At this
moment I don't remember anything. I found myself in my
mother's bed. And There you go. I was robbing him of this
scheme because I no longer lived in my house. She went to
move me without my presence or my consent. I was upset
because I didn't want to live with her. I wanted my
independence.

As if that wasn't enough, she wouldn't let me go out. She
instructed my brother and sister not to give me any keys
to go out. It didn't involve a walk, nor a visit, nor any
fresh air, I was getting suffocated. Every day I shouted
at the inhabitants of the house. I pretended to want to
look for work to go out for a bit, but she refused. She
went with me to go for a walk, to church, to the
hairdressing salon ... It was not the joy. It was too
much, a thirty-one-year-old adult couldn't live like
this. I told myself I had to get away from it all.

One evening she came home, I took the keys from her bag
and went to see a friend of her who was staying at the
hotel. He admitted me but didn't allow me to sleep in his
room. Even at the hotel tonight, I was waiting for help.
All night long I stood in the lobby waiting for someone
to come and help me, but nothing. Then my mother and my
siblings disembark and they force me out. My sister
ripped off my bag without permission. My mother called
the hotel manager to force me out. He offered to put me
in a taxi, but I refused. So he led me outside and I
found my mother. She forcibly pulled me into her car and
took me home. On the way I wanted to go to my father's
house but she did not take me there. We meet at home
around two in the morning. I was badly, and unsatisfied.
The refusal to go out continued until the day she took me
to renew my identity card torn off during my assault.
Before going out I packed my bag for several days. One
morning, we went to the police station for the
formalities. I buried myself when she asked me to go and

get the information from the service in charge; then I went to my father. Everyone was at home. As usual I occupied the strangers' room.

My father arrived at night, found me sitting in the living room. He greeted me with yells, "Go home to your mother! I don't want to handle this! Go to your mother's place ! With my eyes wide open I didn't know what to do. I kept my cool when he went to his room. I didn't know he had a very bad time in his home for me. In his house I suffered his nerves, his aggressiveness. It looked like he was speaking to a ten-year-old girl he had picked up on the way to welcome into his house. I used to stay there though. And his words showed he knew what I was going through. I suffered from his reluctance when I told him about what I was hearing outside, especially the presence of foreigners to resolve the issue. I put up with his screams when he found me waiting for a hand or the planes. I endured his lack of financial support when he gave me taxi pennies with aggression and insults. At one point I had to stop work because I didn't have a taxi fare. Almost every evening this gentleman would ask me to go back to my mother's house, which I could not do given all that I had experienced there. It was horrible he knew everything I was going through as sadness and he chose to behave that way, plus everyone saw him hurting me. I was petrified hence my unease at this house. I avoided it when I could, morning and night. He often put my suitcases outside for me to come home, but I managed to put them back in the house. The final point is when he beat me to get rid of me from his home. One evening he came home drunk and rang the bell at the gate. Seeing that he was insisting and that no one was opening the door to him, I went to do it. He yelled at me, followed me to my room to the bathroom to give me a kick on the cheek, and stuck a fingernail out.

My father arrived at night, found me sitting in the living room. He greeted me with yells, "Go home to your mother! I don't want to handle this! Go to your mother's place! With my eyes wide open I didn't know what to do. I kept my cool when he went to his room. I didn't know he had a very bad time in his home for me. In his house I suffered his nerves, his aggressiveness. It looked like he was speaking to a ten-year-old girl he had picked up on the way to welcome into his house. I used to stay there though. And his words showed he knew what I was going through. I suffered from his reluctance when I told him about what I was hearing outside, especially the presence of foreigners to resolve the issue. I put up with his screams when he found me waiting for a hand or the planes. I endured his lack of financial support when he gave me taxi pennies with aggression and insults. At one point I had to stop work because I didn't have a taxi fare. Almost every evening this gentleman would ask me to go back to my mother's house, which I could not do because of all that I had experienced there. It was horrible he knew everything I was going through as sadness and he chose to behave that way, plus everyone saw him hurting me. I was petrified hence my unease at this house. I avoided it when I could, morning and night. He often put my suitcases outside for me to come home, but I managed to put them back in the house.

The final point is when he beat me to get rid of me from his home. One evening he came home drunk and rang the bell at the gate. Seeing that he was insisting and that no one was opening the door to him, I went to do it. He yelled at me, followed me to my room to the bathroom to give me a kick on the cheek, and stuck a fingernail out. At the same time I was so angry that urine and feces came out of me. I couldn't believe it was the first time this had happened to me. I slept with the bruises and a raised nail. It was so painful. The next day I wanted to go to the hospital, he refused. I had to flee to the nearest health center and called my mother who gave me an Orange Money transfer of ten thousand francs for first aid. When these ladies from the health center pulled my nail out, I felt in a daze and then after lifting my legs I came to myself. The nurse bandaged my fingernails and offered me a bed to rest on. I spent the night there. One morning the second mother of the house, the nanny of the house learned of the course of the aggression he made me, she brought me for the care where the children of the house were used to heal. This center of reference and trust where I took my exams for the second time made me feel so welcome. The father came to see me in the hospital on the first day and on the second day he suddenly came to leave me my bags and sheets, some of which did not even belong to me. I was very unhappy about it. My stay in the hospital continued: Injections, exams,

full body cleansing and that's it. After being stabilized
by the nurses, I regained my courage to look for and wait
for planes and henchmen.

As soon as I got out of the hospital, it was the New
Year. I continued to even claim the money of the month
because I held him responsible for my discomfort due to
his aggressiveness. He had to fix what he had done to me
as a sore spot. One day, I came as usual to talk to him,
he really yelled at me, asking me not to come here
anymore. So I told him about the need to buy a fan, after
giving me the wrong answer, he kicked me out of his
office. It was a straightforward separation.

The most inconsolable of my woes was when I went through
my periods of unemployment. The phone call that would put
me back to work was never given to me. I was penniless.
My savings had been stolen by my mother. And the rest of
that savings was ended up in daily expenses. No one to
help me. It got me days without eating when I lived at
home. I only lived off my mother's meals when she had
time to send them to me. Sometimes she would give me a
few pennies but nothing very important or even enough
that she owed me. She hadn't paid me back everything she
owed me. I spent a year waiting for this phone call from
my job to no avail. I had a really bad time knowing that
I wasn't growing professionally. For a young woman who
flourished through her job it was bad.
Even when I had plenty to do in Bonapriso there, it only
lasted a month and two weeks. Not being able to pay for
my taxi anymore, I had to stop again as he was late in
paying my salary which made matters worse. They never
paid me my month and a half of work after so many
complaints. I was penniless, I didn't live at my usual
pace. I couldn't afford my cleansing milk or soap. I had
turned pale, my complexion had lost its radiance.

From this lack of money I had more complicated plans for
the future. Since no one was helping me, the baby's
father didn't show up. And I admit I had to take Norlevo
to evacuate the fetus. I cried a lot while doing this.
Why had he left me? Why didn't they come out after the
trust I had placed in them? It was very painful to lose
my babies twice in a row because of the awkwardness, the
stress, the noise, the loneliness, the absence of the

father of these children, the lack of means as well. I
felt the joy and sadness of a mother.
I experienced loneliness, my friends were gone, I missed
my job. I experienced celibacy also because of the
distance and the noise of the bandits. Some of my friends
don't speak to me anymore. They miss me a lot.
Friendships that we never imagined could be shaken or
broken have been swept away by the silence. Everyone
mouths closed because of this disaster.

Furthermore, I was amazed and misunderstood by the
stubbornness, unconsciousness and dirty intentions of
some people. With this prevalent connection and hacking
problem that was bothering me, a man with great resources
to fix it surfaced. Incomprehensibly, there were
individuals who asked him not to give a solution. We
spent days convincing the tall man to disconnect, but to
no avail. Discouraged, that's how I still find myself in
this situation.
Faced with all this list of obstacles and embarrassments
crossed, justice is desired and always awaited because
living such a difficulty, discovery of moreover on a
large scale and not being able to drag the perpetrators
to justice in order to put an end to it makes things even
more complex. . It's supposed to end normally. Every day
we whisper that justice will be done. There are indeed in
all countries, the system being normally constituted.
This is what every victim would ask for. All the more so
when it comes to a disaster of this magnitude and this
immeasurability.

Even divine law could not tolerate such obscenities
because the Lord does justice to the oppressed. This is
our God forever. Just as he is the God of the hungry, the
blind, the overwhelmed, so is he those with hacked
brains, electronically connected bodies. Everyone has the
right to their own field of recognition, I claimed mine.
The law of Israel protected widows, orphans, disabled and
I saw my brain, my life disabled so I claimed my divine
protection. My tears flowed that could fill ten buckets
of water. The bible says that the tears of the widow run
down the cheeks of the Lord just as the tears of those
who suffer run down the cheeks of God. I suffered from
it. I would still wait for divine justice to be done. May
that which was trampled from me and taken away from me in

the eyes of Christian law be returned to me. Just as we have witnessed the victory of man over disease, we proclaim a reproduction, a retransmission of these electronic practices. Man and his well-being must prevail over these intentional patients.

<u>**My brain attack by Miss TCHEUKO TCHAPDA MALVINA PRUDENCE.**</u>

THE EFFORTS DEPLOYED AND PUT IN PLACE AGAINST THIS SCOURGE.

On July 14, 2020, I tried to run away. I heard that henchmen were there to rescue me. The idea occurred to me of rushing to the hotel room rented by a good friend and eldest of mine. Here I was waiting for their signal and alert. On television, on TF1 was broadcast the parade of July 14, my sense of respect for colors asked me to great the motherland and the flags. A very well organized parade, spectacular as usual. Thank you.

Always guided by voices, comments from people outside my house. I went to another hotel to wait for them, I could hear the foreign voices speaking in English. I was sitting facing the pool watching this mom who in turn was watching her children swim. It was beautiful. I waited sitting for almost 2 hours without success. I felt them close to me but no one deigned to come out. Go find out why.

Then I got a job, another job. It came at the right time because I no longer wanted to continue in this process. I wanted to concentrate at work and analyze my career prospects. The work consisted of doing the call center and receiving customers.

Even at this job, they wanted to take action. They were talking to me asking me to get out and wait by the side of the road for a car to pick me up. Even when I went to a bakery for me to eat, there was talk of one of them approaching me. Once again, an unsuccessful deployment. It was a shame.

They even colluded to make me a child since I was not yet a mother. In the shadows they said to me 'go to the hospital'. Caught in a trick, I understood that we were talking about an in vitro child. I went to my trust center, during my fertile period, claiming to want to do vaginal exams. At the time of the sample, all went well. Days gone by, weeks gone by, an egg was forming in my stomach. I was pregnant for the second time! I could feel them, there were two of them: twins. I cannot hide from you the joy in the comments when the sample was taken and when the seed touched the egg, the whole process was followed and lived from the inside, my inside, my belly.

Who was the author? I didn't know, at least not yet. It was therefore necessary to hurry, to make quickly and to leave. I was still bleeding, it was a risky pregnancy. So they set up the schedule for the planes to carry me. Every night and morning I got ready to go and wait at the stadium not far from my father's house. I went back and forth every day for almost 90 days with no luck.

  I was still pregnant.

Then time passed, the pregnancy evolved. I chose to pick them up from another hotel as this time it was more critical than before. I thought I could get at least one bag or someone who noticed me. I already knew that I was famous or at least that I was no longer alone. Again, nothing and no one on the horizon.
I still had the babies in my womb.

In order to multiply my efforts and achieve the goals, I decided to go to a hotel located very close to my place of service. It was all about what I heard, too. The news was accompanied by hotel names. I told myself that knowing where to find me, the henchmen would stay nearby just to make our job easier. And so after working hours, I went to the nearest hotel to find out if x and there were staying or had left a room in my name. The feedback was negative, closed. After hours of waiting, I left my contact to let me know when there might be something new. It was by taxi that I took the way back. I remember this exchange of anger as I listened to them talk to me on the way, yet I had waited hours in the waiting room without ever seeing anyone appear. All the way back, I could hear these strangers talking to me. In anger I asked them what I would do with a child whose father I didn't know. A voice answered me and it was very cold.

Also in the deployment I had to travel to a village on the west side to seek protection. I have met healers who through their practice have gone out of their way to protect me. Then we took the way back to my mother, her friend and me.

Still within the budget I asked for help and then received 250 CFA thousands from a wonderful old friend of mine. This helping hand I had asked for from my home in Logbessou. This amount of money helped me with taxi fares and hotel stay. I decided to give it another chance and go stay at the hotel. After work I took a room not far from my place of duty. I spent the night there but to no avail from the henchmen. It was then that may there was no human presence or evacuation process to help me, I chose to remove these children by taking a pill which had this effect. And that was the end of babies.

Also, the idea of throwing myself a bag came to me and I shared with them, here I was in the hospital. Let's say a health center, this center in which I have given all my confidence without ever being disappointed. It was late 2020 and I even spent the New Year in this hospital on medication. As I tell you, I was beaten with a removed fingernail. So being in this trusted hospital, the plan was to throw me a bag with the necessities to use. I could see lights in the sky at night, they looked like airplane headlights. Every morning and evening I waited for them on the veranda of the hospital, on the floor where I was. But nothing, I spent almost 18 days in this hospital with no results from these henchmen.

Then when I left my hospital room, I was already receiving quality care. I was determined to see them, to be done with them because I wanted to leave this country or even touch a solution. I had this idea of going to the nearest hotel because it was also a question of escorting me, of slipping a letter or documents under the door of the hotel room and even of me. Approach at reception. The goal was to get closer to me and together to make a concrete base of contact. I had rented this room for 24 hours. After these 24 hours I had to vacate the room very sad because the operation had failed. I came out with no results from them. So that was the last time I walked into a hotel to look for these goons.
Then when I left my hotel room, I thought of saying hello to an uncle and my mother's friend. I didn't want to go home to my mother to remember the injections I had to have which put me to sleep and weakened my body. My uncle brought me to eat some super delicious meat kebabs. Not knowing where to go, I let myself be led and found myself at my mother's office.

<u>My brain attack by Miss TCHEUKO TCHAPDA MALVINA PRUDENCE.</u>

To my surprise, they still tried to convince me about the injection. They took me to the psychologist who offered me pills and injections. This injection which had the effect of falling asleep and tiring me all over the body. Filled with anger, I refused and left this institute all upset and disappointed.

Arrived at my mother, the deployment continued. The goons always wanted to act. There was a question of throwing me a bag on my veranda and taking me in a chopper at the stadium located very close to the house, located a few steps out. This operation continued and is wanted until this day I hold my pen for you.

At my father's house, some friends and colleagues wanted to participate, I heard that they would come to throw me some money but were prevented from doing so. They were stuck because the timing between my waiting hours and their arrival times did not coincide. Also, looking at what would happen in the **B,** they got discouraged.

My brain attack by Miss TCHEUKO TCHAPDA MALVINA PRUDENCE.

THE ATTEMPTS, THE COOPERATION, THE UNDERSTANDING AND KINDNESS OF THE MEN OF THE SHADOWS.

I was in Bonaberi with my father, I was watching television, suddenly a thin, fine white and transparent light appeared at the same time. This is the closest description to what I saw. A fine glow to which I have attributed a divinatory notion and a spiritual meaning. For the simple reason that afterwards I saw him fight a monstrous evil creature until he disappeared.

Christian intervention had confirmed its merciful supremacy. That glow and transparent white light appearing everywhere I was, everywhere I went. This rather fine glow gave me the impression and the feeling of a spiritual, religious, holy, protective and caring intervention. The most concerned of all. The most beautiful, the most reassuring.

While I saw evil creatures in the sky, this glow intervened.
At bedtime, while I was making my prayers, my novenas, this glow appeared

Everything was so involved, I often even burned incense to purify myself and drive out evil spirits. My mother and father had recommended a priest and a priestess to me, from whom I supplied myself with grains and burning powder. Because who says divine intervention also says the possible presence of contrary creatures or likely to harm. As if to say that this fine light appeared during my privileged moments with incense. These moments during which I asked the Lord for divine protection, infallible throughout this plague. I asked him to find a solution to this problem, also to give strength and courage to those in charge of this phenomenon. Because at that time, I didn't feel alone, these kind men of the shadows were present. This is why, when I prayed with incense, I incorporated them. You see incense granting all your wishes. I highly recommend you give it a go, the results are amazing.

At breakfast, dinner, and supper I felt blessed because that glow flooded me with her presence. It was regular and frequent. That kind of consistency that never annoys you as long as it is protective and memorable.

Watching television too, I was entitled to it. This divine presence liked me, I sensed it. I subscribed even more to watch the programs of the KtO channel. With its most informative shows ever. Both on the Christian faith and on the manifestations and effects of the Lord's presence in our lives.

How do you thank a glow if not through additional prayers and love of neighbor? I found comfort in my live rosary prayer sessions on this same television channel. Through the scenes that were presented to me, the sounds, the external comments, I was aware of his presence and his intervention in other skies. I remember I felt its unifying effect. She was leading everyone towards a common goal, a similar goal, a similar feeling: that of peace, stillness, release from anger and nervousness. But the tumult remained, the criminals were disobedient to it. The noises and arguments continued. It was horrible and very disappointing. What a lack of respect for Christian values!

I would like to shout out the Christian flavors I had to taste. My mother and I deployed these religious means to put an end to these attacks and to claim divine protection from the good Lord. Sometimes I would go to a priest who would give me holy water, then I would go home and bless my whole house in its nooks and crannies. By this time I was home downstairs, lighting incense almost every night, anyway when I needed it. I poured holy oil in my house and at the entrance to avoid evil-minded people. Often times I drank it when my body felt trapped in the evil one. It was after that I knew it was all about the manipulations of bodily connection. Also in this sense, my mother would take me to another priest who gave me a prayer book and then oil to anoint against evil spirits. So I was using this notebook to pray to the good Lord, invoke his presence in my life and throughout this bitter struggle against connection and these evil creatures. I asked him to get me out of there by all means. When I was with my mother, I remember when I had to anoint myself with this oil; after doing it, I felt my hands and feet like animals. Shortly after it was gone, I repeated it twice to see if the results would be the same. Then another day I anointed myself with this palm oil with good results this time. No unpleasant feeling, I understood that this was the manipulations of those who connected me.

There were also the nice shadow players. I will never forget them, these influential men with important charisms, immense kindness, concerned enough to arouse appeasement, tranquility, obedience…. Clearly, they weren't from here. It is with real pleasure and a smile on my face that I hold my quill or pen to relate and describe their majestic intervention. They knew what to do. Endowed with all forms and kinds of solutions for this problem, both in particular and in general. They could do anything. They had authority and strength in the process and solutions, of course they were allowed to respect a framework. They will understand.

Certainly they weren't from here. But there was a homogeneity in their understanding and mine, we vibrated in phase with what needed to be done. The vision was shared. I perceived the ultra concerned about their person. Both for my cause and for the common cause: Peace, calm, common satisfaction.
I heard that I am a billionaire, and that obviously its effectiveness was in progress, the related amenities too. For a billionaire, so much could be done to save her again that the situation was very dangerous.

The Lord allowed me to find a comfort as I watched the Tokyo 2020 Olympics, which by the way were the best I have ever seen. The spectacular side got away from me, away from the worries, the noise and the mess around me and my house. Watching them on TV had the advantage of distracting me from my sad thoughts and the deplorable situation in which bad people had put me.

I found entertainment and comfort in football games, because they mean a lot to me. Every morning in my off-peak hours and every evening after work, I zapped to the football channels and delighted I appreciated these talented people and talents. I had the vague impression that I was receiving messages and words even from television at this time. These kind and heartwarming words. But hey, even my favorite TV shows were a big distraction for me. I'm talking about "Good Doctor", "Friends", "Keeping Up With the Kardashians" , "Doctor house" , "Maman et célèbre" and many more. Their reunion, their very interesting messages, their giggles, their transcriptions of reality escaped my sad thoughts. I always have a good time looking at their products, the fruit of their labor.

Once, I will not forget that. At that time I was living with my father whose house was a few steps from the big stadium. As I tried to sleep on my bed, I heard "I want you to come to my family". Some kind of call or a foreign voice, speaking in another language, in English. afterwards I had the information that he was a footballer.

Once again I had the proof that my life, my difficulties had crossed borders. This kind invitation made me fight. She comforted me, she signified a presence to me, a wanted and desired help. So what to do other than throw the elevator back to him, of course nodding and telling him what we could do to resolve this problem that seemed known and this difficulty that seemed sympathetic.

I had a good time seeing someone on TV and in the evenings I saw them in my room. I don't know how he did it, but I had his shadow sitting on the edge of my bed. It appeared when I was eating grilled fish. He came to support me, to console me. Very kindly, I appreciated him and I shared my meal with him, I also wanted to understand this apparition, I handed him a piece of fish but this piece has not disappeared. Um, I get it. With this shadow we exchanged a lot of discussion and hugging, a single kiss. We spoke in the English language. He expressed his intention to marry me, and I had to follow his instructions, the schedules of the planes that would come to pick me up. After a little kiss, we said goodbye and then he left; and the next day he was there, I followed his instructions to go to the stadium to wait for the plane. I have done this several times without success. According to what he said, there were people standing in the way.

<u>My brain attack by Miss TCHEUKO TCHAPDA MALVINA PRUDENCE.</u>

While I was doing some cleaning plus tidying up. I put away my justFab, Nine West, Tom and Eva, Fendi, Karl Lagerfeld, Boohoo and many more and it gave me a distraction. So I could think of something else and appreciate these designers and their products from big brands. Having their shoes, bag, clothes made me lucky and privileged, because they too were known internationally.
I will not fail to mention the interventions of my friends and acquaintances. They had chosen to act without my knowledge and in the shadows. Also, I have an old friend who gave me money when I needed it most. This amount of money helped me to lodge myself to wait for the henchmen. Others tried to get the police to intervene against those who were making noise around their homes. Still others very kindly intended to come and give me a little financial encouragement because I was unemployed and had nothing in my pocket.

Everywhere I was I received the laughter of certain people. Their laughter for me meant not only that they were paying attention, that there was a hilarious aspect, but also their intention to share in their fun. I had it from the top of my apartment building by a young lady: a feminine laugh. I also noticed when I was working as a call operator, this time the laughter was male. All these beautiful people were present, he found something to laugh about and that had the effect of reducing the drama to perception even if afterwards he returned and resurfaced on a daily basis.

<u>My brain attack by Miss TCHEUKO TCHAPDA MALVINA PRUDENCE.</u>

DENOUNCE THESE ACTS: BRAIN PIRACY.

Before we used to say that you can't scrutinize someone's mind, now it's hard to say that because brains are within reach or the phone. Morals are depraved. We are witnessing a depravity never seen or known before. Or at least it looks like walking naked in the street, moreover one could speak of nudity of the head or open head, naked of body, naked of organs, naked of heart. Even the period of surveillance cameras is outdated. Surveillance cameras are no longer sufficient, they are limited in the face of this device which traces facts, gestures and thoughts.

The impurities, the secrets, the little nonsense, the big ones in others are known by who will snoop around and use this instrument. Who would like to see their heavy past resurface? Especially if you're not proud of it. This may resurface not on your own because you haven't told anything, but because of an instrument and its user. It is the two put together that pose the problem.
I believed that only the Lord could search the kidneys and the heart. So let us leave this care to him, that it remains his prerogative, he is the only divine master.
 Be careful to tolerate this kind of practice: a hacked brain and body and permanent electronic contact is neither convenient nor allowed. It could cause complications following magnetic and electronic contact. This act would be judged tortious and criminal (details can be provided by experts) remains in itself an immeasurable illegality, unforgivable to update, denounce and punish. It is to denounce and repress the firm hand, with the last and greatest energy that it is.

Here is a grid that would show the seriousness of the offense and act through the use of these instruments. We thus trace the links with existing legal qualifications, which attests to the concretization of these offenses and crimes. Of course, experts and tools in the field will make amendments and improvements.

My brain attack by Miss TCHEUKO TCHAPDA MALVINA PRUDENCE.

Acts experienced and observed.	Potential offense qualifications assigned.
Link, connect the human being to the machine.	Human rights violation.
Cross the cerebral boundary to read or insert images and audio.	Brain invasion by electronic way.
- Administering blows, smells and slaps and touching, - Jostling the organs of the body.	Electronic beatings and tortures.
Look in a home or private enclosed space.	Spying.
Send creatures to my home.	Home violation.
Inserting substances and heat into the body.	- Use of illicit products. - Attack on human dignity.
Make noises and comments at home and in any place and watch the facts and gestures.	Breach of privacy.
Use the ideas and thoughts emanating from the brain.	Aggravated theft.

The membrane or envelope that covers ideas and thoughts appears as a limit and would know how to be crossed at the risk of encountering a difficult understanding, or of facing it. I own my flow of ideas. No one has the right to enter and grab it. The discussion remains and remains complementary; It remains the key, the essential solution, the beginning especially to avoid what could invade the nosy (the one who pirates) I speak thus of the interrogation or the questioning, the implication, the anger, the frustration, the misunderstanding, the complaint to name just that.

<u>My brain attack by Miss TCHEUKO TCHAPDA MALVINA PRUDENCE.</u>

I heard he had this opportunity to have a question-and-answer session. Magic! But who had made this possible? Using my head for fun? No, I will never endorse it.

Come to think of it, this analysis that could escape more than one. There is a certain limit when we have individuals opposite who are called upon to converse or exchange. Unlike when someone has your brain and thoughts close at hand, there is a barrier, a measure. This would take the form of respect, politeness, courtesy, chosen ignorance, tolerance or even the choice to be silent which turns out to be another manifestation of respect and many more. These did not seem to appear when you were put on this device with the question-and-answer session. Side-by-side or face-to-face discussions and those on the machine provide two closely distinct results, at least there is a definite lag.
This observed discrepancy aroused, as guessed above, a lot of disagreement creating in each nosy (the one who hacks) an upheaval when this one had an unsatisfactory return both for his self-esteem and in the appreciation of a simple comment given, or a notice raised.

That being said, real life prevailed. The need for normal contact remained.

We could also have nice words, values that shift towards this instrument; Never mind, I am one of those who breathe the idea of giving good and beautiful people the latitude to take responsibility for their beautiful ideas and all that goes with it. Meritocracy prevails. As mentioned above, grabbing it without authorization or mutual consent has an unauthorized side with this risk of disregard or frustration in the event of derailment of an idea, if there is any.

To live through all of this is very difficult.

Even more difficult are the pains I felt when I was undergoing the electronic form attacks. I'm talking about the propelled air, the pikes, the slaps, the stretching of the nerves. Also concerned are the eyes, nose, teeth, neck which were painful when these criminals amused themselves with electronic torture.

My brain attack by Miss TCHEUKO TCHAPDA MALVINA PRUDENCE.

It's not just the head that gets attacked, my whole body is abused and electronically tortured. We reiterate the issue of respect for human rights. They see themselves flouted and harmed. Be connected to an electronic device to endure blows of air, pikes, stretching, pushing and beating on organs. This concerns the arms, veins, bones, back, scapula, breasts, chest, stomach, ribs, nerves, navel, bladder, vagina, thighs, legs, toes ... In short all parts of the whole body and I beg you the words are weighed. The human body system experiences some kind of dysfunction although it is periodic. Never mind, no one has the right to have access to it and to engage in such obscene acts. The human body being sacred.

In addition, reading the profile of these criminals reveals criminal tendencies.

Also , to this abuse, there was electronic warming of the body. Thus undermining human dignity. The latter recognized as one of the fundamental among the individual freedoms due to man. The latter flouted this right specific to man and recognized on an international dimension.

This is how, for example, when I was lying down, by means still ignored, they ran up and down my body, giving me a sensation of electric heat. He is denounced because after this sensation, my body lost its faculties, it became quite tired, impossible to obey. My body could no longer shower, walk, cook, let alone sit still: it was limp, it looked like it had no bones. According to the freedom attributed to human beings, they have the right to dispose of their bodies as they see fit and as they like. That's why it's out of the question for malicious people to come with childish bad intentions to give my body another destination.

One cannot fail to underline the intolerable and inconceivable aspect of the espionage of which I am a victim. For the simple reason that there are things that cannot be shared. The habits and frequentations of the toilets, the actions of the bedroom, the kitchen, the living room. In short, we are talking about privacy.

<u>My brain attack by Miss TCHEUKO TCHAPDA MALVINA PRUDENCE.</u>

The roofs, barriers, doors and windows of a house are no coincidence, it's not at random. They have their place. They should never and could not be ignored. Their purpose and goal are known and are the customs of life. They protect individuals, keeping them safe. It preserves modesty, thus preserving abject images. These roofs and barriers and doors envelop privacy, preventing access by others without authorization. In my opinion, privacy is the foundation of man. Privacy enhances human morale. Privacy is shared only when there is consent, even mutual consent. There are habits and actions that are meant to be behind closed doors. It should not be accessed without permission, such as dating in the kitchen, shower, bedrooms, living room, office, meetings, work sessions and even with family. And therefore crossing and infiltrating in any way into a house or under a roof should never be within reach of bandits and strangers with non-Catholic intentions. A roof is not installed for anyone to walk through, no! Barriers, enclosures, doors and windows are built to enter by knocking, knocking on the door, using a bell. You can and should only have access to a house through these forms. "Knock, knock, knock" or "cling glong". We still have to wait to have agreement and acceptance to cross the threshold.

Very rudely, people went so far as to spy on my household, houses too. This household which has the particularity of being cherished by any owner, thus enclosing my nudity, all parts of my human body, my shower, my clothing choices, my underwear, my privacy, choice of dressers and cabinets, my colors sheets; the frolics of the bed, the towels, my sanitary napkins too, not to mention the times when I use them. They have access to my culinary choices with their preparation and cooking timing; the layout of my kitchen or the kitchen in which I cook myself; the colors of floor tiles, pots, utensils, spoons, knives, forks; the dishes, the arrangement of the fridge and its contents, the bread, the butter, the ham, the meat, the spaghetti, the cans, the potatoes, the plantains, the apples, the juices, the beers, the ice cubes, the condiments, my garlic which I cannot do without because of its virtues. That consumption of garlic that I recommend to everyone.

 In my living room, my actions were watched by I do not
know who and by the large number too, the same for the
location of the living room, the choice of armchairs, the
dining room, my photos, my television, my television
moments, the table, my guests, the meals served at the
table, the discussions and exchanges, the good times and
the moments of argument. It was all within reach.

Please, let us ask ourselves a little bit of a simple
question: if we do not tell you, if it is not the subject
of discussion or sharing initiative, how can others know
all these examples known cited? Please, the recital of
these examples revealing the gravity of the situation and
the excitement of this act of espionage. It is
inconceivable and unacceptable! The point closed, all
that should be repressed. Experts in the field will be
able to tell us how far the penalties can go. Why don't
we talk about electronic break-in? Especially with all
the noise it generated? I think we will have to
contextualize and then update the sentences.

I think specifically that its use should be reserved for
the professional body of investigators and those of
defense secrets.

With this instrument, they have visibility into all the
compartments of the house. They abused when they took
this freedom to comment on what they saw, to talk about
it without embarrassment. Likewise, dawn and dusk were
within reach; bedtime and daybreak were the subject of
impolite and disrespectful phases.
There is this chatter that never ends. Night and day, I
suffered the noise, inappropriate words, vulgar and not
clean at all. My peace of mind is shaken, attacked. I no
longer have peace of mind at home. In the middle of the
night it's the same; verbiage to no end and of a very
useless nature to become so.

I reiterate the absolute and infallible discretion of
what happens in the house or bedroom. The average person
shouldn't go into it in any way, let alone comment on
what's going on, especially if it doesn't offend anyone.

I repeat such a use should be reserved for the professional body of investigators and those of defense secrets.

My actions and actions are described. For example, when I put down an item of clothing I hear outside my house "Look where she has thrown her coat" But damn it! As if I had to explain what I was doing in my room.

Memories are told orally. This electronic uproar was not in conformity with the mores or the classic habits known to all and to which all were accustomed.
So there is the act of pushing a person's ideas and memories with the back of the hand. No one has the right or the authorization to do so. It was safe to stop them and put them aside because they are aware of what they are doing.

Taking the form of harassment, we must denounce and put an end to it. I filed a complaint against that act. I may chase them and scream, but they always stay there continuing their delinquent act. samely, at this level, subject matter experts will be able to tell us what they incur from offenders.

Likewise, they have access to your daily route line. That is, everywhere I went was known and known. I speak of the number of my steps, my crossings of roads, the number of cars that I saw, the posters and the noise of motorcycles… Likewise, in a crowd or in the middle of people, they could see these people like me. Who can live like this? There was only one thing to do and that was to ban the use of this instrument by the masses, and drastically.

Hacking, invading is the property of those I would call intentionally ill. It is therefore a question of treating them.

My brain attack by Miss TCHEUKO TCHAPDA MALVINA PRUDENCE.

THE CONSEQUENCES OF SUCH A PRACTICE ON EVERYDAY LIFE AND ON THE FUTURE.

This practice of cervical piracy and connection of the body I find in it many bad consequences. This is how the head affected by the nerves risks damaging the brain. Several times I have seen myself forgetting what I had done minutes before. I tried to remember my actions but I could not find them. I am traumatized for life. It's like a sense of frustration that never ends. This is the result of the unique and unheard of appearance of this phenomenon on a human being.
Knowing that I am connected is demoralizing because it is invaded by strangers who approach me in a certain way and without my consent. Spied on, seen in my enclosed space, I no longer have any privacy. With the crossing of noises I no longer have peace. Some saw themselves reaching the limit of politeness and sending rambling words to these disorderly people who took turns sowing trouble in the houses.

In addition, a connected person leads to the connection of those who appear in their perceived visual? I mean the people he lived with, the people he worked with. There was a good chance these would also be seen and connected. It took on a pyramid shape that was difficult to escape and stop. And since things are spreading like this, it stoked bad looks, jealousy, bad guys, uprisings since the lives, the pasts, the dailies, the heritages were known to all. These people, although they had done nothing wrong, were no longer safe from malicious glances. Logging in also caused people to indulge in rude words in my head, proliferating name-calling and threats without knowing me.

With the abuse suffered on the body, you risk being weakened, your physical form necessarily takes a hit, with the risks of hospitalization and costs. There is a risk of personality disorders when you are injected with animal products, for example. Twinning connections mean that there are no more boundaries or barriers between human beings. Everyone sees each other and the notion of slyness is almost eliminated. The ways of speaking change, they become leaning; that's when we'll be entitled to "see what she said? Yet before we listened or just heard what the other was saying, now we see them because the writings pass on a machine thus retracing your ideas and your words. Just as connecting people leads to being able to hear everything you say when you pay attention. Also going so far as to create a kind of large-scale interactivity and this without dimensional limits.

With such a device, we see known secrets with heritages and memories past, present and future. I don't know someone who would like to have their whole life opened up to the smallest detail that way. In the future what you plan to do is known, your capital of tomorrow in terms of actions, projects and lived and revealed. Being focused on a connected being, one of the high risk consequences is that you could have your project stolen. I speak of theft because we confirm the ownership and ownership of everything that comes from your head or brain. It is then that these connectors can have your projects, and model them, reproduce them without your consent, and without your knowledge. Which is neither appreciable nor professional. Every human being is a source of inspiration. But as soon as connected, every human being becomes a database. A human being should not be treated like this.
Also, things can be better arranged. The rights recognized to each on what flows or emerges from his brain must be framed. Authorizations can follow, so we can now call, mail, send a contract ....

In turn, the texts and codes could be innovated and updated in view of the new situation of delinquency and criminality. It's so popular that some people are going at it. These are not the practices for the masses. It will therefore be necessary to contextualize the punishments due to new forms of delinquency and attempted homicide.

THE ATTITUDES TO HAVE WHEN FACED WITH THIS KIND OF ACT.

Faced with noise, you have to keep calm, ignore them and continue your daily routine. Failing to keep calm, they must be chased away with prayer. You can also repel them by calling out to other people. If so, this is what happened. The others were trying to talk to them about quitting on the connection or at least not connecting me anymore, the others included.

We must also call on justice. I went to the gendarmerie to file a complaint and I am waiting for the rest. And knowing that everything is verifiable, legal action can follow as usual. We must denounce and repress this kind of acts or all those who adopt behavior contrary to the norms during this disastrous situation which is the whiplash and the connections of human beings.

In the face of physical and neck abuse, the attitude requirement is similar. Either keep calm or chase them away. Chase them by shouting they will hear you because they are connected. I, for example, had to scream, yell for them to realize the gravity of their actions. Of course knowing that it is known to all, I was accompanied by people around who shared the same ardor, and logical idea. If you feel empty in your body due to electronic torture, rush to the hospital for a consultation or check-up. This is important for your peace of mind and your morale. So mass awareness was needed against these perpetrators, forcing them to calm in homes and disconnect from organizations.
On the other hand, in order to protect individuals and maintain respect for human rights, a number of initiatives could be taken. It would start with the establishment of new laws. New standards were to emerge, rules updated and contextualized; justice to be done for the victims of these unforgivable acts.

In order to save the victims, an evacuation process could be put in place. Quite simply by contacting them, writing to them to give them a course to take or a path to follow. Of course a logistic put in place should follow. You could also deploy the planes, the helicopters to take them each to their home or to a site where everyone would meet. This attempt was made for me even though a lack of organization was lacking. Lives were in danger, men and women were exposed to the general public. It is therefore a question of deploying all plausible means to secure or eradicate the danger around us, from me. The obligation of result was theirs, or our seeing that it is already a community in the face of this scourge, this tragedy. So everything had to be in place to save, secure and improve daily life.

Similarly, gadgets and noise-canceling devices could be designed and manufactured. These could close in the sound effects that harm and break the links between the transmitter and the receivers that are homes and people. Or similarly, tools with a somewhat closer purpose manufactured which would prevent the reception of noise on or around you. These initiatives do not come from the extra, so a device and process against disorder is indeed possible.

Living in such a situation requires prayer. Invoke without ceasing and the divine spirit will act. Because the holy spirit is always triumphant.

My brain attack by Miss TCHEUKO TCHAPDA MALVINA PRUDENCE.

THE SONG: Yesterday, today and tomorrow.

Why this silence ?

Just a sign from you. A phone call, a message, a mailing, a letter, WhatsApp, Facebook, a lunch or dinner….

There was an infallible, indestructible base,

Was it her fault? You know for a fact not. No no no you all know it from the bottom of your heart, as in an open book you recognized it.

They nosed around, they committed unauthorized things
You searched, you looked at what was not told or narrated or to share.

But above all they saw that she loved you very much, that she respected you very much.

Chorus: Eyes closed, I see you.

Eyes open, I still have you on view.

Around me your shadow, always your gesture.

Even my sensualities, you searched and found.

Present without being there, Absent and felt.

My senses, my suffering, my joys known and perceived by all.

Over there, yes you know over there.
She heard your voice, your protective voice, and your worried voice too.
Here, she perceived your presence in certain places where she was going.
It wasn't utopian, no
In this Yesterday, today and tomorrow
You weren't dishonest, you supported her, as usual.

Chorus: Eyes closed, I see you.

Eyes open, I still have you on view.

My brain attack by Miss TCHEUKO TCHAPDA MALVINA PRUDENCE.

Around me your shadow, always your gesture.

Even my sensualities, you searched and found.

Present without being there, Absent and felt.

My senses, my suffering, my joys known and perceived by
all.

Everything is tangible, tangible and real.
Everything is known, read, expected and wanted and still
not yet provided.
It was a mixture of surprise, smile, giggles, anger….
Tolerance, rigor I grant you.
But there were unchangeable
You have opted for silence, me on the other hand
tolerance, indulgence I have chosen.
Invaded and enveloped by this power of the clear
conscience.

And what did you do with it the next day?
And where has this well-known tomorrow reading gone?
It's not a medium's initiative, it's yours.
And where is the chouquette? this representation of you
and i. You saw it in this book of tomorrow. Where is she
? where are these children?

Chorus: Eyes closed, I see you.

Eyes open, I still have you on view.

Around me your shadow, always your gesture.

Even my sensualities, you searched and found.

Present without being there, Absent and felt.

My senses, my suffering, my joys known and perceived by
all.

<u>The Song 2 :Thank you</u>.

Angels surround me, I say thank you.
Thanks for protecting from the bad guys.
I was able to have a healthy life, thank you.
For health, kindness, charity, prosperity, loyalty,
thank you.
For my children, my family, our meals, our walks,
thank you.
For the beauty and elegance of my wife, my fiancée,
I thank nature.
I am lucky to have a sister, a brother, a cousin, a
nephew, a niece to whom I say thank you.
Thank you for the kindness of my friend, my
colleague, my teammate.

<u>Chorus</u>: Thank you to heaven.
Thanks to the moon.
Thanks to the earth.
Thanks to the stars.
Thank you to the sky.
Thank you to the paradise and to who else?

Chorus :

I say thank you to the teachings of life.

I thank for my diplomas and my work and my
company, my business.
For my developed talent, I say thank you.
For my salary, my shares, my profits, thank you.
For the gift of my efforts, I thanks the sky.
I say thank you because I trust him, her and they trust
me.

And then I thanks my efforts and my hard work for
my wardrobe, my house, my buildings, my villa, my
palace, my car, my jeep, my truck, my private jet, my
boat.
Thank you for my rewards, my bonuses, my golden
ball.
And so to the sports community thank you.
Thanks to my laughs, my moments of relaxation, my
Joy times, also for my repairs and improvement.
Thank you because I have known love and friendship
Love and friendship
Thank youuuuuuuuuuuu
I thank the sky, thank you and even the colors of the
rainbow.

<u>The Song in French version: Merci.</u>

Les anges m'entourent, je vous dis merci.

Merci pour la protection contre les méchants.

J'ai pu avoir la vie saine,merci.

Pour la santé, la bonté, la charité, la prospérité, la loyauté, merci.

Pour mes enfants, ma famille, nos repas, nos balades, merci.

Pour la beauté et l'élégance de mon épouse, de ma fiancée, je remercie la nature.

J'ai la chance d'avoir une sœur, un frère, un cousin, une cousine, un neveu, une nièce à qui je dis merci.

Merci pour la gentillesse de mon ami, de mon collègue, mon coéquipier, mon confrère.

<u>Refrain</u> : Merci au ciel.

Merci à la lune.

Merci à la terre.

Merci aux étoiles.

Merci au paradis.

Merci aux astres et à qui d'autres ?

Je dis merci aux enseignements de la vie.

Je remercie pour mes diplômes et mon travail et mon entreprise, mon commerce.

Pour mon talent développé, je vous dis merci

Pour mon salaire, mes parts, mes bénéfices, merci.

Pour le cadeau de mes efforts, je remercie le ciel.

Je dis merci car j'ai confiance en lui , en elle et ils ont confiance en moi.

<u>**Refrain :**</u>

Et puis je remercie mes efforts et mon dur labeur pour ma garde-robe, ma maison, mes immeubles, ma villa, mon palais, ma voiture, ma jeep, mon camion, mon jet privé, mon bateau.

Merci pour mes récompenses, mes primes, mon ballon d'or.

Et donc à la communauté sportive merciiiiiiiiiii

Merci à mes fous rires, à mes moments de détente, à mes Joy time, aussi pour mes réparations et amélioration.

Merci car j'ai connu l'amour et l'amitié.

Amour et amitiééééééééééééééééé

Merciiiiiiiiiiiiiiiiii

Je remercie le ciel, merci et même les couleurs de l'arc en ciel.

For any use of the copyright of the songs, contact us at +237 699 1769 07
Or by email via tcheuko.26@gmail.com
Or on facebook: MalvinaTchapda
For operations, they will be done through the account:

UBA BANK From Cameroun.

CODE BANK: 10033

CODE AGENCY : 05201

N° Account : 01068011904

CLE RIB : 18

Swift code : UNAFCMCX

IBAN : CM21 10033 05201 01068011904 18

I want morebooks!

Buy your books fast and straightforward online - at one of world's fastest growing online book stores! Environmentally sound due to Print-on-Demand technologies.

Buy your books online at
www.morebooks.shop

Kaufen Sie Ihre Bücher schnell und unkompliziert online – auf einer der am schnellsten wachsenden Buchhandelsplattformen weltweit! Dank Print-On-Demand umwelt- und ressourcenschonend produzi ert.

Bücher schneller online kaufen
www.morebooks.shop

KS OmniScriptum Publishing
Brivibas gatve 197
LV-1039 Riga, Latvia
Telefax: +371 686 204 55

info@omniscriptum.com
www.omniscriptum.com

Printed by Books on Demand GmbH, Norderstedt / Germany